A
Patchwork
of
Comforts

A Patchwork of Comforts

Small Pleasures *for* Peace *of* Mind

Carol Wiseman

CONARI PRESS

First published in 2004 by Conari Press,
an imprint of Red Wheel/Weiser, LLC
York Beach, ME
With offices at:
368 Congress Street
Boston, MA 02210
www.redwheelweiser.com

Library of Congress Cataloging-in-Publication Data
Wiseman, Carol.
    A patchwork of comforts / Carol Wiseman.
      p. cm.
    ISBN 1-57324-904-1
    1. Pleasure. 2. Stress management. I. Title.
    BF515.W57 2004
    646.7—dc22

2003027387

Typeset in Electra and Papyrus

Printed in Canada
TCP

11 10 09 08 07 06 05 04
 8 7 6 5 4 3 2 1

My gratitude to . . .

The love of my life, my comforter Bill, who
encouraged, contributed, . . . and loved.

My children Christy and Jesse, whose flexibility
with life is a constant reminder to lighten up.

All who responded to my survey—your serious
thoughts made this book possible.

Diane Harwood for firmly pushing me forward:
"You have to start this Monday. I'll call to make sure
you do." She did, and I did.

Don Bishop, whose early thank-you call let me
know I could make a difference.

Table of Comforts

Welcome

The word pleasure *has such a gentle, smooth sound to it. It's a word that makes your mouth feel good when you say it, and the images it opens up always make you smile.*

This was the first sentence I wrote in a paper on pleasure for my first writing class many years ago. It seemed like a fitting start to a book on comforts because the words *pleasure* and *comfort* lace together so gently, like the strands of soft yarn in a winter scarf.

From that first descriptive sentence my imagination took off. Just think how much different our lives would be—calmer, happier, healthier—if we spent more time nurturing ourselves and less time on the endless string of tasks we assign ourselves every day.

To broaden my point of view I asked everyone I knew, past and present, about their personal comforts by sending out a letter asking, "What comforts you the most?" and "How do you relieve your stress?" The results were a treasure trove of ideas. As replies trickled in, my excitement over every single one led my husband to speculate that I'd invented a new tactic for getting more mail, the kind with my name written on the envelope in real ink.

Surprisingly, this small sampling turned out to be a broad cross section of feelings and dozens of positive solutions to life's pressures . . . plenty of fodder for my book. There was a commonness to comforts, a similarity of individual techniques. One thing is sure: it proved that we all share the need to be nurtured in some way.

My most memorable surprise was the night my husband's godfather called. He had recently lost his wife, and my request had prompted him to spend time thinking about their last year together. Writing out the details for me helped him to move forward in his life. That night he called to thank me and to tell us how much better he was feeling. It was an unexpected turning point for me. This project now had new meaning.

With my letter in hand, people were forced to think about what comforts they had in their lives. Results were surprising. Some realized for the first time that they never paused long enough in the day to ever feel that relief. Three women confessed that thinking about what pleasured them actually eased an ongoing depression; thinking about any good times had stopped for them long ago.

Responses varied in detail but themes were common; a lot of you are either walking, reading, cuddling, eating, or daydreaming. My personal favorites: "The best thing about doing nothing is resting afterward" and "Taking off my bra at the end of the day." Dylan said, "Only eating Goldfish makes me feel better." (He was four and loved crackers.) My own favorite thing: Not being in a hurry.

The result of my survey letter is a personal book with a simple, lighthearted approach that's designed to ease your day and give you new ideas for dealing with stress and getting more pleasure out of life. There are no wordy explanations or dialogue that demands interpretation; just a collection of observations on what people think and the places they go — sometimes just in their own minds — when the details of their lives get them down.

Reading people's responses about what comforted them most allowed me to glimpse into secret worlds of relief. From their brief descriptions, I created two perspectives from which to view each comfort. The first is drawn from my own imagination and is written in a first-person voice that will pull you gently into each experience. The second is made up of my own thoughts on what makes each subject a source of such pleasure. Each different comfort will transport you to a respite from your everydayness. My fondest hope is that you'll get some good ideas to integrate into your own life. Reading *about* comforts, after all, should *be* comforting. Enjoy. . .

Alone Time: The only voice you hear is your own

Chris, from Grants Pass, Oregon, clears her head by escaping her work world on the weekend.

It's Saturday and I'm heading for the hills. Five long, noisy days of being surrounded by people—who kept talking and expected me to talk back—is over. By Friday night I felt like screaming, "Leave me alone, please!"

I've been labeled shy all my life, but I'm really not; it's that small talk I'm no good at. You know, the stuff people say just to fill the silence. The reason I love the mountains so much is that chipmunks and birds don't expect anything. They go about their eating business and leave you alone to listen to what's really important—buzzing . . . chirping . . . trickling.

Being alone gives us time to think more clearly, when we're not constantly reacting to warm bodies all around us. But balance is tricky. Working people who are surrounded all day crave more peoplelessness, while retired seniors who stay at home most of the time hunger for the opposite.

Alone time is merely a breather for socializers, who love that human connection, but it's vital for those of us who absorb the energy of people around us until it feels like electric current running through our bodies. At some point we're desperate to break away.

Alone is different from lonely, when we yearn for more company. And being "a loner" describes those who like it that way most of the time. We tend to label them antisocial or "too big for their britches" when they don't join in. Maybe it's just that their tolerance for chaos is low, or maybe they were celebrities in a previous life.

There are ways to insulate ourselves amid the hubbub without resorting to the mountains or a desert island. Putting a canopy over our bed creates the illusion of being in our own little world. It has a low roof that separates that space in our mind and designates it as special. We automatically sense its privacy and safety, and we feel cozy in our nest. A special sitting corner in our garden, a B&B out of town, or a bath before bed all designate "our own space" and our very own pint-sized R&R.

"Alone" lovers: Escapees from the constant static of people and their expectations

Aromas: Trigger memories

*Dena, from Grants Pass, Oregon, calms down
when her favorite smell drifts by.*

Wow, the sweet smell of honeysuckle. Halfway through
my morning walk today I turned the corner to a wonderful surprise. The air was filled with honeysuckle. You
can't see it, but your nose knows.

At about the second block I began to notice how tight
my neck and shoulders were. My jaw was tight, and I
was frowning. I was sure that if my neighbors drove by
they'd think I was mad at them. This was supposed to be
a time to unwind, but that mental list of the chores I had
to do kept running 'round and 'round in my brain. By
the time the honeysuckle was done with me, my face
was relaxed. Same with my mood.

Smells hit unexpectedly. We could be typing a report
or taking our morning walk when suddenly there's
a familiar smell. First there's recognition, then reac-
tion. The memory smell of Mom's chocolate cupcakes brings
a smile, but the cologne an old boyfriend wore makes us
squinch.

Most smells, good *and* bad, grab us just because they're familiar, like morning coffee, roses, puppy, seaweed on the beach, or outdated milk. Everyone agrees on the great smells like cinnamon rolls in the oven or lilacs in bloom, but some good smells can be bad, like the sweet fragrance of sweet peas to an allergy sufferer and the pungent smell of axle grease is heaven only to mechanics, and old car buffs.

The same nose that detects a gas leak in the house detects romance from roses in the room. And just imagine the inside of our cars and homes if we couldn't detect doggie-doo on our shoe.

Aroma: Silently alters your train of thought

Nothing says "Welcome to my home" like the scent of fresh-baked bread or chocolate cookies wafting through the house.

Bath: Ahhh, alone at last

Carol, from Grants Pass, Oregon, depends on her hot bath to soothe her mind and body.

I am a bath addict. My world of comfort starts when warm water engulfs my body, where a small room of unspeakable pleasure brings relief from the angst of life, from cold toes and cluttered minds.

It's February and I'm chilled to the bone. A day of details is finally over. I head for the back of the house to fill the tub—nice and full, nice and hot. Not enough to scorch body parts, just warm enough to melt the day.

I light a candle to balance on the rim of the tub and put on music that's barely there. Pulling the curtain to wall off the rest of the room completes the stage for this daily renewal. I step in and sink down . . . slowly. Ahhh, my eyes close automatically as the wonderfulness surrounds my body.

We're alone at last. This door can be locked, away from the phone, children, partner, obligations. With scented candles and soft music, relief is complete, magically transporting us to a little bit of Eden.

A hot soak slows body and brain to a crawl, winding a day of hassles down to zero. Warm water surrounds every muscle, as if Mother Nature herself were cuddling it and saying, "Relax, everything's all right now."

Ohhh, the pampering. At this moment *we* are the most important person in our very own sanctuary. It's a time to savor, since these do-nothing moments come rarely in an active life.

Bath: Liquid relief engulfs us.

Bed: Human nesting

Pan, from Wolf Creek, Oregon, turns to her bed as the ultimate healing place.

Dragging myself out of bed today is harder than usual. My throat burns and my joints ache, both signs that a cold is coming on. It doesn't seem bad enough to call in sick, but by noon I regret my morning decision. Coworkers are glad to see me—and my contaminating ways—leave early. As I hit the freeway to home, I begin to think about my bed, my wonderful, wonderful bed. Suddenly the car takes off on its own, as it heads "back to the barn." Clothes come off before I get to the bedroom, where I pause just long enough to take two aspirin. Bed is calling. I wrap myself up in the down comforter and scrunch it up under my chin. Tomorrow will be better.

Bed is where we want to be when our body's feeling lousy. Being swaddled in a fluffy comforter soothes us with a healing power all its own. It's why people take to their beds when they're depressed, or just sad for the day.

Beds feel safe. Lying in the dark and the quiet, listening to soft rainfall on the roof, feels snuggly, like the hugs we got when we were four. And if sprinkles turn to thunder, pulling the blankets up to hide our head makes us feel protected.

Personality quirks emerge at midnight with twitchers, snorters, talkers, walkers, and those who steal blankets every time they turn over. Gentle sleepers quietly spend the night in one position, as if their dreams were a good book.

Beds are magic carpets, taking us to places we want to revisit again and again. And sharing the details of a crazy dream before we get up starts off the day with a good laugh, although figuring them out can take a master's degree.

Bed = Nest = A place to dream, heal, hide,
read, whisper, and make love

Howard Hughes designed a bed for himself with thirty electric motors, to move himself and various parts of the bed. He equipped it with piped-in music and hot and cold running water.

Birding: Finding flying treasure

For Sue, from Burlingame, California, spotting a new bird and adding it to her "life list" is very exciting.

When our neighbor moved he didn't want to haul the concrete fountain in his backyard to his new house. He hadn't filled it in three years anyway, so he offered it to us. Actually, it looked like a giant birdbath, so we filled it, and then waited. I thought it was too deep for birds to use, and wanted to put a big rock in the bottom for them to stand on, but my husband said to wait.

Three weeks went by—nothing. Then tonight, as we sat on the deck in the pitch dark, we heard splashing. We knew birds don't bathe at night, so I ran in to get the flashlight. We couldn't believe it. A pair of small owls, maybe 8 inches tall, sat on the edge together, taking turns swimming across the bowl. I guess they were bathing, but we will be telling our friends they were swimming.

The bright light in their eyes didn't faze them at first, but 30 seconds is all we got. We'll be out there again tomorrow night . . . waiting.

Catching nature off guard peaks our wonder. Most of us are too busy earning a living, commuting, parenting, or doing household chores to notice that we lost the automatic curiosity of our youth years ago. The closest we get to interacting with fauna is when we head for the toilet carrying our latest conquest, a mashed spider in a tissue.

Backyard birders arrange their furniture in front of windows so they can keep track of local visitors, while serious seekers, searching for eagles in the wetlands, politely argue over species. Each side finally decides—in their own heads—that they are right.

Auduboners are a special breed. They flock to field trips, where enthusiasts are decked out with the essential binocs and ID book. Bird watching to them is more than just relaxing; it's a game that demands 100 percent of their attention. Can I find a new one before it finds me? And when I do will it perch long enough for me to remember specifics? The challenge of spotting a "new bird for them" is to be quick, identifying as many body parts as possible before flight. Substituting a camera for binoculars assures that their friends will believe their find this time.

Creeping is essential, whether it's sneaking through backyard grass or in a car-train of birders. As they inch in as close as they dare, they alert each other over walkie-talkies. It's when telescopes are set up to look them in the eye—for the big ones that linger—that begs the question, "Who's watching whom?"

Country livers have lots of opportunities, but even they are often too busy to pause and appreciate the giant, red-headed woodpecker on the old snag at the edge of their property, or a male mourning dove watching out for his sweetie down below.

Audubon marriage: Never having to argue
about where to go on vacation

The Amazing Woodpecker

Tail feathers bend and spread to form a tripod with its feet, buttressing it against the trunk as it hammers for a meal. Two toes in front and two in back allow it to grasp firmly and balance on vertical surfaces. Cartilage between beak and skull acts as a shock absorber for its battering ram. As its beak probes insect tunnels, a very long slender tongue with a barbed tip scoops up insects with the help of a sticky substance that coats its tongue.

Breathing: More than just oxygen to your brain

Blake, from Sunny Valley, Oregon, induces calm by taking deep breaths.

Until today I thought breathing was what I did naturally. After all, I'd been doing it since I was born and never once had to think about it, except for the time when I was learning to snorkel and had to hold it longer than I thought I could. True, I knew it was harder to breathe hiking up a slope, but I also knew that breathing faster happened without even thinking.

I went to the bookstore to check out the blue book value of my car and got distracted. There's a whole shelf of books on breathing. I'm too curious to not notice so I pulled one out and sat down to read. How could you write a whole book about breathing? What more is there than "in out, in out, in out"?

Turns out there are different kinds of breathing, and since there was no one in the aisle to see me, I tried one out. Inhale through the nose fast, hold, and then exhale slowly through the mouth. It was true, I felt more relaxed after doing it five times, as if I had just exhaled all my worries. Well, not all of them; I'm still trying to decide whether to trade in my car or sell it myself through the classifieds.

Isn't this why we call it the autonomic system? Our bodies are built to breathe automatically for us. Why should we spend our time thinking about it?

The drill goes something like this: Stress makes us tense our stomach muscles. We revert to shallow chest breathing, which increases fatigue and tension. Deep abdominal breaths help turn off anxiety by stretching and relaxing the diaphragm, giving us more air. Our brain then signals our whole body to release tension.

Smokers know. That first deep inhale is so relaxing that eyes automatically close in ecstasy. But the American Lung Association says it's the deep breaths, not the nicotine, that does it.

A Great Breathing Exercise

When work stacks up on your desk, pick up a pencil. Hold it lightly with the pointed end between your thumb and fingertip. Then get comfortable, close your eyes, and slow down your breathing. When the pencil drops, you are totally relaxed. Savor the feeling for a few minutes.

(Adapted from *The Daily Relaxer* by Matthew McKay and Patrick Fanning.)

Camping: Leaving cement behind

*Elizabeth, from Rogue River, Oregon, finds
peace camping in the woods by herself.*

The key to my weekend was not hearing a single phone
ring. Actually, there was no noise at all except some water,
owls, and our own footsteps as we walked through the
woods.

My wife and I set up camp as fast as we could. We
pitched the tent and set up our nest inside it, organized
the food for the next two days, and decided where the
"rest room" would be. Then we set up two cots side by
side outside the tent, threw pillows on one end, and
flopped down to look up into the trees. We were free to
do whatever we wanted, whenever we wanted to, for two
whole days.

After an hour, we got up to investigate where the
sound of water was coming from. We wound in and out
of the trees, avoiding clumps of poison oak, until we
came to a small creek with a log-bridge across it. We
walked to the center and straddled the trunk, dangling our
feet 6 inches from the water. As it flowed over some large
boulders, I closed my eyes and could almost hear the
sound of my grandfather laughing but trying not to. This
chuckling should put us to sleep just fine tonight.

Another hour there and it was time to break out the beans and franks (the only nutrition we brought was carrot sticks). Back to camp to eat, watch for chipmunks, listen to birds, and whisper if we had to. No time for anything else; too busy smiling.

It was two glorious days of hearing nothing but owls hooting, crickets cricketing, and water tumbling over boulders.

Getting away from civilization is its main draw. Escaping the cars, buildings, cement, people, and whatever noise and requirements they bring, guarantees a 20-point drop in our blood pressure. Here, we're as free as the birds we are watching. Relaxing is a requirement.

Before we enter this other zone, decisions need to be made. Choices exist these days beyond throwing a sleeping bag on the dirt and using our saddle as a pillow. Camper or tent? Cot or not? Pad or plain dirt? Pillow or wadded up sweatshirt? TP or leaves? Deciding how far back-to-nature we want to go dictates packing priorities.

RVers practice cheater-camping, packing the latest *TV Guide* and heading for a public park where neighbors are still 20 feet away. Serious nature lovers carry the essentials in their backpacks and hike to where few humans have been, hoping to feel the thrill of that survival mode. Camping separates men from mice in bear country, as they waiver between hiding their garbage or their heads, or staying up all night with cameras ready in case a photo op shows up.

Once decisions, planning, packing, and driving are over, and we mingle with nature, we realize that here's a place where the food tastes better, drinks refresh quicker, and the morning sun seeps into our bodies like it never did at home.

Real Camping

No: TV, phone, blow dryer, panty hose, makeup, shaver, watch, mirror

Yes: A good book, holey T-shirts, sweats, toothbrush, flashlight, hiking shoes

Candlelight: Mellows the mood

*Donna, from Grants Pass, Oregon, lights candles
whenever she needs comforting.*

My bath has become an "event" ever since I discovered
how to get rid of that glaring overhead light; candlelight
is all I need to avoid groping for the tub in the dark. I
found a small candle shop in town and now have a collection of pink, green, and blue candle cups that hold
my favorite scents, such as vanilla, lemon, and coffee
cake. A special place is cleared on a shelf to display them
all so I can pick one to match my mood every day.

Tonight it's blue. I light up, sink in, and let my senses
flow. Suddenly there's just me and flickering and mellow.
The soft light shimmers on the water above my body, as
if I've captured moonlight in my lap.

Candlelight mellows moods. It's hard to stay grumpy
after a hot soak next to the tubside glow of candles.
Candlelight mellows circumstances. A party lit with
only candles avoids that awkward "warming up" period that
happens when lots of people who don't know each other get
together in one room. No icebreakers are needed; dim lighting

brings smiles and conversation to guests right away. The easy atmosphere is because guests know all their flaws are hidden for the night.

Candlelight softens faces, giving us a temporary facelift. It's why candles are good gifts for those of us who can remember how our faces looked before they were road maps. It's why dinner by candlelight defines romance; inhibitions fade when we know we're beautiful.

Candlelight: A good substitute for makeup

Homemade Mirror Ball

Paint a cardboard box silver and cover with large silver and gold glitter. A stiff cord inserted in the corner allows it to hang off kilter. Line furniture tops with candles, and the walls explode with sparkles.

Children and Family: Knowing they're well is everything

For Cynthia, from Grants Pass, Oregon, stress evaporates when she remembers what's really important to her.

Whew, my boy's going to be OK. The relief I felt today is the kind you get when the fright of your life is finally over and you can breathe again.

My son loves his bike. All day long he rides up and down the street with a neighborhood friend who likes to take chances. This morning I got the phone call every parent dreads: "Aaron took a header off his bike." When the pounding of my heart stopped, I heard the words *bike* and *ramp*. Just riding back and forth, it seems, got boring. Making a ramp would liven it up. Oh, yes.

Seeing my six-year-old lying in the ER with two black eyes and a huge knot on his forehead broke my heart. But the news was good. It looked worse than it was—just a mild concussion. I exhaled at last.

And now my baby's grown

I hadn't seen my son for more than a year. Oh, we'd raised him to be independent, and knew that he was happy from phone calls, but it just isn't the same as touching. I longed to put my arms around him again.

Today was the day. They wouldn't be here until after three, but I couldn't concentrate on anything else and spent most of the day walking back and forth between the kitchen and the big window that looks out onto the driveway. I thought maybe his favorite meat loaf would make him feel at home again. Finally, the car. I hurried to the window just in time. Watching him, his wife, and my brand-new grandson get out of the car made my heart pound. Wow, he had a beard this time.

Me hugging him made everything better. I have to remember the laughs, the stories, and the catching up we did today, because it might be another year until the next time. I wanted to know everything, from diaper rash to mortgage payments. I hope they don't think I was too nosy; I was just so anxious to hear all the news in their lives.

Some of us are lucky. We can count on family—to offer an ear, a shoulder, or the wisdom of slip-ups over the years. And even though our grown children have their own homes, they live close enough so we can still exchange daily details and birthday meals. Close families stay connected even if they live 2,000 miles apart and only see each other every five years.

That connection is easy when our children are young. Contact is constant. But when childhood is over and they move out on their own, details are harder to grab. Their lives get as busy as ours were at the beginning, and contact with Mom and Dad seems less important than it used to.

In the beginning, before having our own children, we noticed that parents never leave home without the essentials: diapers, tissues, and protective clothing. At this point in our lives children are defined by spit-up, drool, and constant leaking . . . from everywhere. Then comes our own. Suddenly none of that matters anymore. Suddenly their spit is our spit, as if we are blended.

All we hope for when our children are very small is normal development and a good night's sleep. As they grow up, discover the outside world and start exploring (on their bikes! Yikes!), we pray they look both ways, pay attention in class, and feel good about themselves. By the time they're ready to move out from under our wings, we hope they'll make good wages, drive slower, and remember to make their own appointments to the dentist once in a while.

In the end, we want our children to have more than we had. We want for them more money, more contentment, better health, and more of whatever they want in life. We raise them the best we know how to at the time, watch them learn their lessons like we did, and hope everything turns out OK by the time they're grown up. When it does, relief is constant.

It's so much fun when our grown children come to visit, just so, every once in a while, it can be like it used to be.

Just listening tells your children they matter.
It helps you understand their point of view.

A Good Family Formula
Hugs + kisses + talking + listening + laughing

Collecting: More is sometimes better

*Tom, from Henderson, Nevada, revisits his youth
whenever he looks through his collection.*

What can I say, I love bulls and bears. I grew up in
Chicago so being a Bulls and Bears fan is a natural. And
I wanted to quit working before I was fifty, so, coinci-
dentally, I took on the bulls and bears of the stock market
to pay the rent.

Visitors think I'm nuts. My whole office is devoted
to my teams, with every bit of memorabilia I could accu-
mulate over the years. Scotty Pippin's number 33 jersey
hangs next to a Bulls banner on the wall facing the door.
It's the first thing you see if you get the grand tour of my
house. On the wall to the right is a large tree form, with
the names of all the Bears hanging from the branches.
Next to it is a picture of Mike Ditka and Walter Payton.
A wall cabinet to the left is filled with little stuff, like
fishing lures, steins, key rings, pencils, mugs, paper-
weights, and labels that were cut out of the player's old
sneakers. On the wall next to the cabinet are two frames:
one has belt buckles and the other holds an arrangement
of lapel pins.

I have a vest, suspenders, tie, robe, slippers, shoelaces,
calendar, lamps, pencil holder, mouse pad, bookends,

watch, clock, pencils sharpener, rubber stamps, glasses, erasers, and an assortment of figurines—all with my teams' names on them. I bought wallpaper once, but I just taped it up so I could take it with me in case we moved.

I wouldn't want to be without my teams; every day I get to remember my youth. What can I say, I love my room.

Collectors are a species that take great pride in owning "the whole set" or "more than anyone else." They travel thousands of miles in the name of the hunt, then glow as they show off their finds to visitors. They get great satisfaction from filling in the gaps—like finding the missing pieces to a jigsaw puzzle—and seeing this orderly array of treasures on shelf after shelf after shelf.

This clutter isn't clutter to them; it has a theme and matches each other. You can't really count it as junk; after all, it's not a hundred "stuffs," it's just one . . . large set. But sets do collect dust, and there's plenty of that in designated rooms; collectors and sneezers have a hard time living together. Display cabinets with glass doors save the day.

Amassing is the goal in this treasure hunt . . . or rather obsession. Collectors start with something they love and add to it whenever they run across a variance. Pretty soon it's all they get for birthdays and anniversaries, until they're known simply as toad woman or the hat lady or just plain Crazy Pete.

Africans collect goats; Americans collect cars.

The Washington Banana Museum is home to 4,000 artifacts devoted to America's best-selling fruit.

Confidence: Courage to take a risk

Suzi, from Rogue River, Oregon, feels great satisfaction with the choices she's made in life.

My friend Debra talked me into taking a self-defense class with her. I always thought that these classes were for shy women in big cities where perverts hung out in alleyways. I only agreed to go because she didn't want to go by herself.

We practiced simple ways to surprise attackers on the first night. None of them required strength, which is why I was afraid to go in the first place; I never thought I was very strong. I found out that simple things could save your life: relaxing "out of" a grip, jabbing vulnerable spots, and making noise.

Tonight was our fifth class and we role-played. A padded attacker surprised us, and all we had to do was escape any way we could. Punch, grab, poke, scream; I did it all and surprised even myself. This wimpy woman pulled it off—for real—and I am pumped.

At first I thought it was the adrenaline, but now, a week later, I realize that for the first time in my life the fear is gone. I don't mean just the fear of men; I'm not as anxious about a lot of things. I even started a conversation with my boss, and then asked for a raise. The sky didn't fall; he didn't throw me out, or fire me. He just said he'd let me know. My God, nothing bad happened!

Confidence is a seed. Once it sprouts and is nurtured, it grows. Knowing we can physically take care of ourselves changes the way we think, and makes us take a second look at our lives. Our fears become more apparent, jumping out and forcing us to pay attention. And knowing we're good at something—anything—gives us worth in our own mind.

Those of us who were raised by parents who believed in us—and told us so—need only our inner voice to say, "Job well done." But most of us crave that stamp of approval from someone else now and then. A raise, a compliment, or pat on the back gives us the confidence we need to feel better about ourselves.

Kids who never got their parents' approval spend their lives seeking it from everyone else. Most of us are somewhere in between, feeling good about one thing while being terrified about another. Plastic surgeons and therapists thrive on our lack.

Lack of confidence holds us back. We're afraid to even try because we think we'll fail. But for confident people, failing doesn't matter, trying does. They trust themselves. Their lives are full because they say *Yes* to last-minute getaways, karate lessons, and screamingly loud Hawaiian shirts.

Confidence: Permission we give ourselves to try

Cooking: Delicious therapy

Margie, from Benicia, California, is contented in the kitchen, making up new recipes and trying them out.

After salivating over cookbook photos this morning, I decided on chocolate cake with creamy chocolate frosting, topped with walnuts halves. I was practically tasting it in my mind when I remembered—fat . . . sugar . . . calories. I ignored all those nasty thoughts because my taste buds had already lured me to the kitchen. It had been a month since dessert.

I laid out all the ingredients, got the bowls and mixer ready, and turned on my favorite cooking music. One-person dancing always makes it taste better, as I mix it up, pour it out, and then snake my tongue between each beater blade. I discovered long ago that a rubber spatula works best for getting every last drop off the sides of the bowl; wouldn't want to waste a drop of chocolate. While the cake is in the oven I make that smooth, dark frosting to dribble over the top. Creating a design of walnut halves on top crowned a masterpiece that even Martha Stewart would be proud of.

Skipped dinner tonight.

Maybe our comfort has less to do with cooking than it does with eating, both the finished product and the tasting in between. Or maybe it's the inventor hiding in all of us; the kitchen's a great place to feed a creative spirit. Fiddling with ingredients keeps the eager eaters in our family from getting bored and entices them to the table faster, depending on our track record of course; the memory of past disasters always lingers longer than we want.

Cooking is cathartic. Chopping veggies counts as therapy when you imagine familiar faces on them first. The chopping block is a good substitute for a face-to-face standoff.

Time in the kitchen makes moving into a new neighborhood easier. Bake something unusual, such as rum coffee cake or fresh sourdough bread, and include the recipe when you take it next door. It starts a good relationship.

Some of us yearn for a homemaking wife of our own. Imagine walking into the kitchen, sitting down, and eating a meal *not* prepared by you. So this is what it feels like to be a man. A good meal is "the way to everyone's heart."

A note: If you can get your honey into the kitchen
with you, kisses make cooking better.

Lemon Curd Tarts

1 cup (8 tablespoons) butter, melted

2¼ cups sugar

5 eggs, beaten

3 lemons, juiced and strained

Rind of 2 lemons, finely grated

Mix everything together over low heat. Stir constantly until sugar dissolves and curd thickens. Let cool, then fill individual mini tart shells.

Cuddling: Back to the womb

Judy and Don, from Sutter Creek, California, end their day by cuddling up in bed together.

I rushed through the dishes when I heard crackling in the fireplace; didn't want to waste a minute of that fire. Oh boy, no one's in the "fireplace" chair. I called "dibs" and raced back to change into my new flannel pajamas. After diving into my favorite chair, I curled up my legs under me, pulled Grandma's afghan around my feet, and turned out the lamp. Oops, forgot the hot chocolate. . . .

When frozen puddles surround the house, and the crackling calls, tucking ourselves into a womblike space feels fine. Curling up in a cozy chair that hugs us from behind reminds us of delicious hugs from Mom. Ever since we left her womb, we keep trying to climb back in.

Snuggly, cuddly, cozy are all words we use to describe that feeling of being nurtured. They're words we all love to strive for, even men, though they won't often admit it out loud. A lover's arms are lucky to have, but goose down works great in the middle of a cold February night.

Is it the warmth of the fire that draws us into bliss, or are our roots still showing gratitude for inventing it?

Dance: Frees your spirit

Rebecka, from Grants Pass, Oregon, floats around the room at the end of the day to spin off her stress.

After moping around for years because the love of my life just sits still when there's fast music playing, I discovered how to satisfy my dancing urge without him — housework. Besides, itchy feet help ease the pain of mopping, vacuuming, laundering, and cooking over and over . . . and over.

Cher, very loud, commands me to move, whether it's the dishes or dust bunnies. I have no choice, because my feet start moving all by themselves. So I wheel out the vacuum, crank up the volume extra loud, and aerobicize. I hate to think of what I look like to anyone peeking in the window who can't hear the music. Just call for the men in white coats.

Dancing lets us express, whether it's pressing bodies close, or just us and the vacuum. The exercise cracks open our pressure valve, as if sweat loosens the latch. Just think about all the pressure that's released in the mosh pit at a rock concert. Maybe this is a good thing after all.

Dancing helps romance along. It gives us a good excuse to move in close, to touch the one we care about when we're too scared to say how we feel. And when we're alone, twirling around a room lit only by candlelight frees our spirit, transforming a workday mode into a weekend mood.

Ballet or tap takes years of sweat, but just a few lessons can start us line dancing or doing the tango, two-step, or hula. Our dance of choice depends on whether we can find a partner who can move their feet to the beat—random shuffling and toe stepping don't count—or if we even want one. Even chair dancing satisfies that dancing urge.

Warning: Dancing on tables at the office party can be hazardous to your health . . . and your paycheck.

Dance: Body contact without commitment

Dark: Mandatory eye rest

Kathy, from Grants Pass, Oregon, sits still and closes her eyes for 10 minutes to ease her tension.

It's 5:00 A.M. and I'm up. Admittedly, it's taken a long time to get used to getting out of bed this early—I used to call it middle of the night—but going to bed at 9:00 P.M. the night before made a huge difference.

The idea of getting up before I had to seemed ridiculous at first, but after I did it for a week it was my favorite part of the day. It's the only time I get to be alone (the kids are still asleep), and I love it. The dark feels like a soft blanket around my shoulders, which is a feeling I protect by turning on just enough light so I don't have to feel my way up the hall or smash my toe on the leg of some furniture . . . again. Once I get situated with my first cup of coffee, I turn off the last lamp in the house.

That kind of dark where you don't need to close your eyes—pitch dark—shuts out the visual chaos. It's when eyes get to rest, giving brains a chance to slow and thoughts a chance to unjumble. Having nothing to look at blocks distractions, and if a migraine's closing in, dark helps it to heal.

Conversation even feels different here. It's a safer place to open up; no one can actually see our face. Some things are just better in the dark, like the whispers between lovers, ghost stories, or bonfires on the beach.

Some brains get more fertile in the dark. This writer gets more inspirations in a candlelit bath, lying in bed at night, and waking up before dawn.

Dark: When the stars celebrate

Daydreams: Going to the movies for free

Kelly, from Phoenix, Arizona, escapes by letting his mind wander.

I saw a woman on TV last night who had just won the lottery—$78 million. Her excitement was catching and started my own mental spending spree. First, book a flight to anywhere. Next stop, the Mercedes car lot on the way to see a contractor about remodeling the house. Oops, did I forget to write my resignation?

Wait a minute. Remodel? Am I crazy? The fact is I don't know how to think big. I'd move, of course, and watch contractors build the house of my dreams.

After 30 minutes of self-indulgence, I started to think practical, like keeping my win secret from money grabbers, or getting a financial planner to make it last as long as possible. (Maybe a new car wouldn't hurt.)

I was swimming in dollar signs until I came to and remembered . . . can't win unless I buy a ticket.

ndulging our imagination lets us wallow in fantasy, as if we were starring in a Hollywood movie. Pretending, if only for a little while, gives us a break from the routine of our lives. Some of us, however, are too practical to linger on impossibilities for long. Short stories flash through all the time, such as: "What if I never had to cook again?" or "How would it be to go on vacation and stay as long as I wanted?" But plot lines are always plausible and seldom list what to do with millions from the jackpot.

As children we're not encouraged to escape into make-believe very often. Oh, it's OK to have an imaginary friend—our parents even pretend with us—but looking out the window during class time is out. Mostly the constant message we get from everybody is, "Get responsible. Get responsible. Get responsible."

If we allow ourselves, daydreaming frees up our uniqueness. It's where creativity is nurtured. Letting our mind wander into places that seem unthinkable lets in new ideas . . . new possibilities.

Daydreaming: A mental vacation to anywhere you want

Dogs: Your children wearing fur

Peggy, from Cave Junction, Oregon, relaxes by hanging out with her dog.

My dog, Rosy, takes the blues away. Feeling sorry for myself is impossible when my best friend is always so happy to see me.

Everything went wrong today, starting with an accident ahead of me on the freeway. Traffic slowed down to a crawl, making me a half-hour late to work. I was behind schedule before I walked through the door, and my manager's already lousy mood got lousier. (A fight with his wife, no doubt.)

No time to prepare for a 9:00 A.M. meeting, too many calls to make. One out of six calls had a human voice; I left messages for the rest. Everyone called back during my meeting. . . . Let the phone tag begin. The copier chewed up my master, I forgot to save a report that took an hour to write, and during break I discovered the empty TP holder at a crucial time.

Coffee was cold, Coke was warm, donuts were stale. I was in my car heading home by 5:02 and pulled into the driveway at 5:45. There she was. In spite of my day, I had to smile. Good old Rosy was racing toward the car, tail wagging dog. She didn't care how work had been. I didn't even have to tell her. The only thing that mattered to her was that we were together again.

Spot loves fiercely. He loves us no matter what and faithfully greets us with a passionate tail wag every day. His trust makes us want to trust back, so we share things with him that we're too afraid to share with humans.

Spot works hard. He sees for people who can't and sniffs out cocaine for cops and coons for hunters. He tells us to check for strangers and bites the ones who get too close. We depend on him to protect our children. In fact, sometimes Spot *is* our child.

Everyone has a dog story to tell. My favorite is told by a friend who waited by the window at midnight for a week, peeking through the drapes to confirm the source of giant piles on his lawn. He religiously scooped up these daily hazards for a week, crept up, and carefully placed the full bag on the owner's doorstep. It sounds like a comedy routine, but it's true. And it worked.

The downside of dog ownership—the poop, complaining neighbors, vet bills, occasional leg humping, and constant sprinkle of dog hair on the furniture—gets lost in the slobbery greeting we get every time we open our door.

The Pekinese was used as a winter hand warmer in seventeenth-century China. Believe it or not . . .

Doing Nothing: Gives your senses a rest

My son Jesse, from Seattle, Washington, likes to shut his senses down at the end of the day.

Lights are out. TV's off. It's time for bed, but wait. As I sit and pause in the stillness, I notice that something's missing. I can't hear, can't see, can't smell . . . anything. Stopping the day's progress, and letting my senses rest, creates a space for the calm. It's been forever since I took the time to do absolutely nothing.

Our senses deserve a rest. They're bombarded every day with too much to see, too much to hear, and too many things to do. The trouble is, as a culture we demand visible proof of time well spent. We use labels such as "lazy" or "slacker" to describe those wise souls who pause to put their feet up.

We admit to feeling guilty when every minute isn't filled. After all, there's so much to do. We're constantly being asked, "What did you do this weekend?" because our friends expect action all the time. We're afraid they'd label us lazy or worse—

boring—so exaggerating anecdotes from last night's party or a trip to Mexico gives us plenty to say, keeps them laughing, and increases our approval rating.

Resting our senses gives our brains a break; this happens automatically when we sleep. When the anxieties of the day before evaporate with the 6:00 A.M. buzz in our ears, we've got to wonder what really goes on in our brains at night. Dreams are mysterious enough . . . now this.

Brainrest allows the dust to settle. Cells regroup, mending perspective and getting ready for the next day's onslaught of data to sort through. But sleep isn't the only rest an anxious mind can have. Just breaking the cycle—fixing dinner, leaving town for a day, or listening to someone else whine—allows our brain a fresh start.

Tending our brain is vital because brainwork—the invisible activity—is the very best thing we do. Where would we be without the thinkers . . . to invent, create, and inspire? We'd be freezing our hinnies in the outhouse at night, throwing spears at woolly mammoths, and using one-millionth of our brains. Then again, we'd also be talking face-to-face instead of e-mailing.

Interrupting daily routine by doing nothing
brings a fresh perspective.

Eating Out: No decisions, no cleanup

Pat, from Grants Pass, Oregon, relishes this break from cooking.

What to have . . . What to have . . . Every night it's the same old story. What can I make in 15 minutes? What will the kids eat? What's in the fridge?

But this night is going to be different. When my husband leaves for work this morning, he says, "Want to go out tonight?" The man knows not what he's just done. He has no idea the impact those words have on me. Dirty bathrooms, errands, taxi service — none of that matters now. All that matters is the light at the end of the day.

E ating out is different from what it used to be. It's so common now that working couples go out every night, taking that luxury for granted. But for traditional homemakers, who see cooking as their duty, restaurants are a welcome break from the kitchen. Believe it or not, there are still plenty of men who, reluctantly, "take the wife out" only because it's her birthday or anniversary time . . . again.

Restaurants mean more than just relief for the cook in the family. The booth in a corner is where lovers exchange sweet nothings. It's where families come to celebrate birthdays or to teach toddlers their public manners. And when martinis are served, eating out means business schmoozing and contract signing.

Budget doesn't matter because we have a huge choice; we can order burgers or filets, beer or champagne, or we can choose a place that plays Mozart in the background or has video games in the corner.

A young husband spotted this sign beside the entrance to a restaurant twenty years ago: "We give our chef a night off once a week, doesn't your wife deserve the same?" That sign changed a grateful wife's life. Like clockwork, she got a night's reprieve, a night to anticipate all week. It was a guaranteed night of togetherness once a week, and she cherished it.

Restaurants: Godsend to frazzled homemakers,
breadwinners, and young lovers

Feeling Useful: Helping someone means you're needed

Isobel, from Grants Pass, Oregon, finds comfort in bringing comfort to others.

Today there are twenty-five people in line when I pull in at 2:45. They're all waiting for the 3:00 P.M. opening of the food bank, all hoping we'd unlock early. Passing out food boxes to people who don't have enough was my new volunteer job.

I'm surprised that the couple I'm helping are both in their seventies and full of energy. They're troopers who've been doing this for twenty years. Roy does the paperwork, walking down the line-up of families, signing up new ones and getting the ages of their children. This helps Arlene and me fill grocery bags with a three-day supply of food, because families with small children probably need diapers and baby food. The choices of what we can put in the boxes depend on community donations, and today there's a rare box of small M&M bags to include for the children. By 4:30 I'm pooped, but not my partner. She's still laughing and going strong. I'm embarrassed, because Arlene is twenty-five years older than me.

The closet-sized room gets hot, but the expression of gratitude when we hand over supplies is heaven.

Doling out food to someone standing in front of us gives poverty a face. The need is more obvious, more urgent. We sympathize with those who are struggling, and empathize by imagining how we'd feel in their place.

Whole organizations are set up to fill obvious needs, such as shelter, food, abuse, or mental care. But sometimes help comes in softer ways. A short note of appreciation or a phone call at the right time is just what some of us need to get through hard times.

We don't have to donate our time in a big way or do it with flare. Just paying attention at the grocery store opens opportunities to help. Short shoppers need help getting pimentos off the top shelf, seniors can't read price tags, and men wander around aimlessly, trying to find a special brand of beans that their wife put on the list.

Just imagine what the world would be like if we all tipped the gas station guy, called a shut-in, or smiled for no reason at all.

You can make a difference in somebody's life. Fill your head with someone else for a change.

Flowers: Nature smiling

Judy, from Grants Pass, Oregon, feels appreciated when she gets flowers.

I can remember the first time a florist stopped in front of my place. I'd seen that van before, in front of other houses, and always tried to imagine what the occasion was; somebody was thinking of someone in a very special way.

I was trying all morning to ignore today's birthday, but now the van is in *my* driveway. The gloom of being a year older faded as I watched the driver get out and walk around to open the back doors. She reached in and cradled a large bouquet of yellow and white daisies. Only one person knows my favorites, and he'd just made my day. The "Thinking of You" card was the best warm fuzzy ever. Happy Birthday to Me!

Flowers dress up our lives in a dozen ways. Red roses tell us how important we are to someone special, and a bouquet of anything is a welcome relief at the end of a pouty day. The wonderful scent of a large and very old lilac shrub demands a whiff, and the spectacular sight of an arbor weeping with wisteria takes our breath away. The first spring crocus signals the end of the worst of it, and a birthday bouquet from Mom and Dad says, "So glad you were born." Then there's that huge pink dogwood on the way into town. Everyone knows that tree.

Flowers can also trigger sneezing fits and itchy eyes and trips to the doctor. But in the end, can you imagine the world without them?

Bravo to the dinner guest who brings a handful of thank you's from her own garden.

Freedom: Your time is your own

My husband, Bill, from Grants Pass, Oregon, smiles every time he thinks about time being his own at last.

The countdown is over—retirement is here at last. Forty-two years of working means I paid my dues and can stop punching the clock. I even bought a special calendar to have the pleasure of putting a giant red X through every single day until this moment.

Just driving down the road is different now. I watch all those responsible people driving to work with a smile on my face. In fact, I love to watch other people work. They're out there, I'm not. It's heaven.

Our budget will be tighter, but the relief makes up for it in a hundred ways. My wife asks me what I'm doing today, this first day of non-work. "Anything I want to."

Feeling free has to do with age. There's the kind that comes with retirement, after a lifetime of relentless pressure. And there's the kind we have in the beginning, before commitment, before house, before children. In between, we grab an hour here or there, savoring those morsels like the crumbs left on our plate from a nice thick slice of devil's food cake.

Feeling free has to do with circumstance. Average Joes think money will give them freedom from worries, but the rich are keeling over from the pressure. Working parents on a merry-go-round dream of being free just for the evening, while childless couples yearn for the responsibility that babies bring. Teenagers want to be free from nagging parents, and we all want to be free from illness, anger, fat calories, and wrinkles.

Friendship: Someone to share your joys and sorrows

To Pam, from Merlin, Oregon, good friends are like money in the bank.

I was dying to tell someone my news. Today I landed the perfect job and was bursting with joy—too much for me to handle by myself. I drove toward my best friend's house on the way home from the good news. Please be home, Judy. Oh great, there's her car. All I had to say was *"Yes!"* and there was dancing in the street, or rather on the porch. Good news has to be shared. My joy doubled.

Best friends feel the ups and downs of our life as if they were their own. They celebrate our joys and cry with us over heartbreaks. Best friends feel safe to us because we know they'll still like us when they find out "how we really are." We can trust them with our insides because we know they won't laugh at us when we confess secret fears and hair-brained ideas.

Mostly friends communicate well. And you can always tell the close ones. They have the guts to tell ugly news—bad breath, boogers, and other unspeakables.

The best friend to have is you.
You're always so handy to yourself.

Golf: Challenge in paradise

Jerry, from Los Altos, California, escapes to the course every chance he gets.

The trees and acres of green take my breath away. Relief begins even before I get to the golf course—four hours with nothing else to think about but golf. Everyone else is working, but I'm here, in the silence of the course. The only sound I can hear is the *thwack* of club meeting ball.

As I walk up to the first tee, I wonder if today will be a career day. Sometimes that first hit tells you how the rest of your game will go. Contact is solid on the first tee, so I'm hopeful.

Keeping track of my ball reminds me of those Easter egg hunts when I was five. Today my little white egg hits the bunker, but a good sandie gives me a birdie on #4. These shots are rare so I'm celebrating . . . inside. Dilemma on #5; a small flock of Canada geese are in the line of fire. Should I scare them off first, or will they have time to scatter after I tee off? I'm going to chance a shot over their heads. It works! What a shot! Now I'm hoping my lucky honkers will follow me around the course.

All in all, it was a good game. Now back to the clubhouse for a beer and playback of each hole with my partners. Great day!

Golfing is so quiet. The only sound you hear is club whacking ball and an occasional cheer for a long putt. The exercise, business schmoozing, and the chance to tell "fish stories" are only side perks. Just being on the greens is what really counts. And golfers count on it every chance they get.

They're focused. They're addicted. The only thing that's on their minds is smacking a small ball into a small hole that's too far away to even see.

Every game is a challenge. Because a fight with their spouse can happen before tee-off, golfers start each game in a different mood, which makes every round unique. Each hole has its separate identity in a unique setting of green, green, and more green.

A.M.'s good; it's invigorating to tee off the dew. P.M.'s good; the pink sunset sky reduces the green of the trees to mere silhouettes. Let's face it: Anytime's good for golf.

Odds of a hole-in-one: 33,000 to 1

Holding the club properly is the most important first step in learning golf; take lessons from a PGA golf professional.

—Ed Fisher, Teaching Professional, Quail Point Golf Course

Good Cry: Our emotions melting away

*Judy, from Grants Pass, Oregon, lets tears
break the tension.*

The kids would be upset if they saw me crying, and I'd
have to find a way to explain why. That's the reason I've
always locked myself in the bathroom to do it silently.
But I'm tired of hiding and stifling the noise. Even before
I had children, I was embarrassed if anyone saw me
crying. The trouble is you always have to explain why.

Today I waited until the school bus took off so I was
alone in the house. This time no hiding in the bathroom,
sitting on the toilet and muffling sobs with my hands.
Today I lay down on the bed, looked up at the ceiling, and
let it go. Usually I'm careful not to mess up my makeup,
but this morning smearing mascara didn't matter. I
squinched my eyes tight, and didn't bother blotting any
tears away. Because I'm usually so quiet, the noise that
came out surprised even me.

The biggest surprise was that after five minutes I
suddenly stopped. I didn't decide to quit and didn't gradually quiet down. Suddenly, I just didn't feel like it anymore. My body must have been done.

If crying is so good for us, so cathartic, why do we work so hard to hide it? Women hide in bathrooms, children hold it down to be brave, and men become experts at swallowing the lump in their throats. Mostly, we teach our sons that men don't cry.

Seeing pain in others reminds us of our own, so it's easy to cry with an emotional friend. Sharing tears means we know what they're going through. The emotion that comes when our own inside hurt builds up—and graduates from moist eyes to downright ugly—purges us. The contraction of our gut just pumps the poison right up and out our eyes.

Movie Theater: Where the masses gather to silently clench their throats and secretly dab away the evidence

Good News from the Doctor: The ultimate relief

For my mom Irene, from Tacoma, Washington, hearing the doctor tell her not to come back for six months makes her heart sing.

I hadn't noticed any lumps on my neck for a long time, so I was hopeful, but I was afraid to hope at the same time. Surely those tormenting chemo sessions must have done something; the constant nausea, hair loss, and weakness had to count for something. The fear of being bald forever disappeared when I felt the stubble, but today's appointment was another story. Today I found out if it was all worth it. Today I found out if the cancer was gone.

As I sat in the waiting room, there were butterflies in my gut instead of nausea. The CAT scan was over, results were in. Waiting seemed like forever. And then I heard the word I was too nervous to even think about, *remission*. My God, a reprieve.

Cloud nine described the way I floated home to share the news with my family. They were waiting at home for me today.

Good news from our doctor means a giant sigh of relief—what a heavy load off. The biggest sighs are reserved for cancer scares, emergency rooms, and everything in between. But people breathe smaller sighs every day. "I'm finally pregnant!" or "Whew, I'm not pregnant." Some news makes feeling bad worth it—like having chicken pox and hearing, "Stay home from school for a week." Not needing that shot after all, getting the cast off, and hearing, "You can go home tomorrow" all bring satisfying smiles of relief.

Best news of all: Your HMO has agreed to pay for it.

A good night's sleep and a morning walk will help boost your immune system and prepare it for whatever the day may bring.

Hammock: Grown-up cradle

Carol, from Grants Pass, Oregon, eases into her body-swing to relax.

That hammock's been calling me for two weeks now, but I've been too busy during the day to lie down. It looks just like the catalog picture, strung out between two oaks in the backyard, so today I finally accepted its silent invitation. It was Sunday morning—blue sky, 75 degrees, not a breath of wind—and I went out to maneuver myself into what seemed like a very tippy place. Once I centered myself in the netting, no problem. The only sounds I heard now were the peeping and fluttering of birds.

I felt camouflaged there, under the blended leaf canopies, and pretended the birds couldn't see me. It worked. Pretty soon I heard the slapping of bird wings on the water as they took turns in the birdbath I bought last winter.

Unbelievably, a little bird landed on one of the wooden bars attached to each end of the hammock. I lay paralyzed, barely breathing, and pretty soon three chickadees were perched 6 inches from my feet. For those short 30 seconds, I blended with nature.

Blood pressure must have dropped 20 points in that hour of calm.

That birds could mistake a hammock for a branch seems impossible. They're so skittery at the slightest movement, and never take a chance of being bullied by a bigger bird or caught by some neighborhood cat. Maybe wearing tree-colored clothes is the key—gray pants, green T-shirt. And the paint splatters left over from a household project can transform our bodies into the tree they're looking for.

Hammocks do come with standing frames for treeless backyards, but suspending them between trees—so you get to lie beneath the birds and squirrels—magnifies the "hammock experience."

Instructions: Getting in is tricky. The secret is holding on to the edge and reaching in far enough with your butt before you drop down. Otherwise it shoots out from under you and boom, you're on the ground in nothing flat. Once you scrunch around slowly (think canoe), get your whole body centered and be very still. After a minute or two, swinging reduces to a very slight sway, just enough to rock you into a nap; a little pillow is essential for this. Stare straight up through the leaves for a while, then close your eyes and relish.

If there's a third tree close by, grab a low branch and pull it just enough for a slight swing. If the tree's too far away, tie a rope to it, and hold on. If you're lucky enough to have a birdbath or feeder, face it and be very still. In a while the birds will forget you are the enemy.

Mayan Indians first made hammocks from the bark of the hamack tree in Central America 1,000 years ago.

Hobby: Calms mental static

Dorothy, from Palm Springs, California, focuses on her hobby to get her mind off herself.

Today I got to work in my yard. Saturday means the working for wages is over and I get to do what *I* want to do for a change. Now that it was the weekend, I was off to the nursery.

Planting a dogwood was my project for the day. I wanted to duplicate the spectacular display up the street, but I was so pumped I forgot to ask how old the neighbor's tree was. (Found out later—twenty-five years!)

After getting planting instructions and potting soil from the nursery, I wrestled it into the bed of my neighbor's pickup and drove home—very, very slowly. The size hole the nursery told me to dig looked like a small swimming pool when I was done, but I rolled the tree into the middle, where it set like an island, and tamped dirt around the root-ball. The final step was soaking while I stood back with a smile and wondered, How could planting a tree no bigger than me have taken so long?

I was beat, satisfied, and noticed that I'd had only one thought all day—that doggone dogwood. I couldn't even remember what jammed my brain the day before.

The temporary respite we get from focusing on a pet project or hobby squashes the mental flitting we do all day long. The total absorption gives our minds a chance to slow down and regroup for the next day's onslaught of information.

Computers signal us when they need more memory, but brains just keep trucking until *bam* . . . heart attack, ulcer, mental ward, or worse. There are so many decisions, meetings, phone calls, runny noses, and errands in one day. There's just too much of everything.

Workaholics claim the opposite, but most of our brains yearn to pause and regroup. A hobby offers the diversion our minds need to slow down to a crawl. And the pride of "I did it" when we finish a project brings with it a sense of accomplishment, whether we're planting a tree, playing a game, finishing a good book, or rebuilding an engine.

Hobby: Brainrest

I Love You's: "Sweet nothings" are reassurance that you matter

Linda, from Grants Pass, Oregon, cherishes these warm words.

I used to think that all he cared about was his job, his next meal, a golf game, and exaggerating stories to his buddies. I was wrong. I was surprised. In between, he thought of me . . . more than I imagined.

Those little fanny pats I get sometimes are his silent "I love you's" and always make me smile. His thoughtfulness breaks my daily routine and says, "I'm thinking of you." What more is there?

An "I love you" from out of the blue lets us know we matter to someone besides our mom. It's nice to hear the words, but a pat, a night off from cooking, or just asking, "How're you doing?" says it all. Just taking the time to ask us how our day was, and then paying attention to the answer, says, "I appreciate you." Daily chores can bury us— there are hundreds—but it's all worth it when we know, for sure, that someone really cares.

Men who are the main breadwinners in a family think that bringing home the bacon should let their wives know how much they care; words are sometimes hard for them. Women like to be reminded; words come easier to them. The meshing of these perspectives makes plenty of grist for the therapist's couch.

Enhance romance. Light a candle, turn out the lights, slip a favorite—romantic—CD into the player, and enjoy.

Jacks on Queens: Black on red fills your mind

My husband's cousin Paula, from Fremont, California, unwinds with the familiar motion of laying cards out for solitaire.

When the dishes are done after dinner, I like to play cards. I've been playing solitaire for so many years that by now the moves are automatic, but that's what I love. My biggest decision is which black king to put the red queen on.

The other is which deck to use. There are three in the kitchen junk drawer, so I can pick the one that fits my mood every night. I bought a new deck last year, but new is too slippery and clean; the cards always slide off each other when I get going too fast. I know the only way to get them old is to use them, but I don't want to because they're too slippery. I guess I'll be using the old ones until the numbers wear off.

The *slap slap slap* as I lay out the cards signals "my time," to me and to the rest of the family. It's when I sometimes remember my dad, who taught me the game forty years ago. When we played together we told stories, solved problems, and laughed a lot. But it's different for me now; I just want to be left alone.

Tonight I could hear one of my boys sneaking up behind me to add his two cents as usual, "Red nine on black ten, Mom." I turned with the "look." He got it. He was gone. Then it was *slap slap slap* once again.

If we had a partner, we'd have to think; we'd want to win. But with solitaire, mental energy slows down and adopts a cadence as we separate the deck into a seven-card lineup across the table. Going out is the goal, but not going out keeps us coming back for more. Beating the deck too often would get boring.

Playing cards makes us stop the motion of the day. Sitting still and concentrating on these two simple things—red or black, numbers 1 to 13—induces a thinkless zone that helps us get a good night's sleep.

We can play solitaire on the computer, but it's just not the same as shuffling that old worn deck of cards, where memories of those who dealt before still linger.

Kitties: Purring = Cat comfort

Carmen, from Medford, Oregon, gets a lift when her cat jumps up on the bed to cuddle before she gets up in the morning.

I've never had a cat, and this week I discovered what I'd been missing my whole life. The only thing I ever knew about cats was that the neighbor's beloved Fluffy killed the birds I loved to feed and left surprises in the garden for me to dig up or sit in. This experience made sure we never got one.

We'd been in our new house about a month and finally figured out that the people who sold it to us didn't want to take their cat when they moved. We already knew that petting or feeding would mean it would never leave, so we tried to ignore the constant presence of a gray cat on the patio. After all, it might be visiting from the neighbor's house. How did we know?

We weakened after three weeks—the whining of a six- and twelve-year-old did it—and let "her" in (a neighbor pointed out that "its" very fat belly couldn't be from eating too much). My daughter decorated a cardboard box right away, cut a door out in front, and printed "Maternity Box" on it. Boom, next morning at 7:00 A.M.

a sleepy twelve-year-old heard teeny peeps from the laundry room and woke us up.

We were hooked instantly and named our new pet Cleopatra, Cleo for short. Watching this process—squirming, mini meows, fighting for nipple space, and, finally, wrestling—brought daily joy to all of us.

Watching where we step is constant, but so is laughter. Our world of fur began.

Kittens on toilet paper packaging makes sense; it's an obvious marketing choice if you've ever snuggled cat fur. It's a tough choice, though—kitten or baby's bottom? They both squirm around and are full of surprises, but there's no denying the velvety feel.

That independent air of cats, that I'll-come-when-I'm-good-and-ready attitude keeps cat owners challenged. Apparently, cats are confused about who's boss. In fact, they brag about being human-owners and compare their humans when they get together with neighborhood friends.

I hesitate to show bias, but have to. Even though the sloppy kisses of Rover massage our egos, give me purring over a bark-fest any day. You miss that tail-wagging exuberance, but the dainty hygiene habits of felines make up for it a hundred times over.

You'll never find a dog in the top of a tree for
three days, waiting for the ladder truck.

Cats hate sticky feet. Upside-down contact paper, with
the edges folded under to secure it in place, creates a
threshold they won't cross.

Learning: Finding mental treasure

My daughter Christy, from Mill Creek, Washington, finds a new perspective by critiquing her own thoughts.

Today I went from room to room looking for a comfy place to sit and start my new book; not a chair in the whole house felt right. For the first time I realized that all the furniture I'd ever bought was because it looked nice. Apparently, it was for show only. I don't remember ever asking myself if I even liked it; I must be nuts.

After spending the day looking around my house for what seemed like the first time, I put a "sell" ad in the classified ads. As soon as the matching stuff goes, I'm going to buy some that I love, and that's comfortable for more than 10 minutes at a time. Whose house is it, anyhow?

When we're twelve, learning means school. It's something that our parents force us to do, and it hurts sometimes. Most of the details we learn there, such as the Latin name for toad genus, is wasted on us, but we'll remember the big stuff, such as Einstein, or WWII, or the president's name. By the time we're forty-five, nerves prevent us from re-enlisting in college classes, where we think everyone will be smarter than us. But most learning comes from the daily experiences we automatically absorb. These are the tough lessons and come harder to those of us who have to get burned three times instead of just once.

Some of us love to learn. Our eyes are always wide, so insights come often. We crave the unknown becoming known and are constantly looking for better ways to go through life. We love to ponder new ideas and are on the lookout because it's so satisfying to catch a truth. The trouble is that all those discoveries make us look back on what an idiot we've been in the past, so we have to forgive ourselves for not knowing better before.

Life is constant revelation. Two-year-olds discover that screaming gets them anything they want. Mom will do anything to stop the noise. When we're twelve, we notice that boys aren't as bad as we thought. And at twenty-two, it's a revelation that the fridge doesn't replenish itself automatically. At thirty-two, we wonder how such a tiny little baby could turn our life upside down, and at forty-two our sixteen-year-old reveals to *us* that we're not a teenager any more.

The urge to learn is so strong. Imagine a seventy-year-old man who finally admits to faking it for sixty years and wants to read for the first time. Imagine the courage it takes to fess up and then to master phonics . . . kind of like a mental Mt.

Everest. Getting hooked early nurtures a curiosity that lasts a lifetime. Going through life wondering—about everything—keeps synapses firing.

Insights: Gems that change your direction in life

Hidden heroes of teaching—our children—teach us honesty, patience, time management, and how to play again.

Letters: Treasured gifts in the mailbox

For Susie, from Los Altos, California, hearing from a friend is the highlight of her day.

I never rush to the mailbox. Why bother? The number of ads, catalogs, and credit card ploys I toss into the trash unopened is mind boggling; eight envelopes in a day usually means there are two to open. Add those to the monthly bills, and you know why I don't wait for the mailman.

Today was different. Tucked between six envelopes bound for the round file was a return address I actually recognized. Wow, a letter addressed to me, in real ink. I'm so hungry for something personal that I rip it open right then and stand in the street by the mailbox, reading my letter from someone I haven't talked to in more than a year. And look at this, a photo too. He probably doesn't know what a difference he made in my life today.

write, so what can I say? Long-winded letters, little how-you-doin' notes, or letters to the editor—I relish them all. Most people I've known, however, don't share this enthusiasm. The only explanation for this epidemic dread of writing is to assume that most of us were traumatized by our high school English teachers. (For my ease with words I thank Mr. Malarkey, freshman English teacher at Los Altos High.)

A quick card from our children or a newsy letter from a friend both say, "I'm thinking about you," and that's what is important. Getting a card that touches our heart or funny bone always lightens the load because mattering to someone is all we ever want. And when we're scared to say important words out loud, we can write them down in a letter and mail it . . . or not. Those are called therapy.

Then there's e-mail. It's short, free, and only takes a minute. This is great for business, but for those of us who are still stubbornly attached to actual paper, the mailman is still a welcome sight.

E-mail versus snail mail = Quick shower
versus hot soak

Lists: Let you know where you stand

My accountant, Stu, from Grants Pass, Oregon, relies on list making to keep things in perspective.

The season is approaching. One month to go before clients start flooding my desk with shoeboxes stuffed with receipts, and spinning tales of how "the dog ate it"(just some accountant humor).

It's tax time again and I'm ready for my annual ritual—scrambling to clear the decks before February. The number of things I have to deal with before the phone calls begin has reached epic proportions. So today I lived up to my accountant stereotype and inventoried. I meticulously listed every single task and could see immediately that some of them would only take five or ten minutes. Now I knew where I stood, which I always love.

Seeing our obligations on paper makes the difference. Like solving an anagram, unjumbling our thoughts into an orderly list helps us focus on one thing at a time. Thinking about it all at once can make us crazy.

Transforming the pressure in our heads to a visual helps us be more objective and takes away uncertainty. Now we can see how doable it all is. Half of the ten things fighting for space in our brain is five phone calls that will take less than 30 minutes, and three of the errands will only take an hour if we plan our route ahead.

For perfectionists, the all-important list prevails. The need to accomplish—and have proof—rules. Unfinished tasks hang over their heads, nagging to be completed. This feeling, foreign to procrastinators, is a vicious circle—erase one, add two. Those of us with the need to accomplish are constantly adding to our list, with the conscious goal of reducing it; this isn't possible of course. In our youth we fully absorb the "work before pleasure" credo, but seldom get to the pleasure; we're too busy constantly tying up loose ends.

Being caught up is only a dream in households where both parents are working. Their list of tasks never ends; there's never enough time. It's as though our brains are automatically set to the "enlarge" option. Why else would it constantly blow everything out of proportion?

List making: Better than drugs—relief is instant.

The Best List of All

- Finish reading this book.
- Pick a new comfort to you.
- Try it.
- Buy it again for a friend.

Losing Weight: Controlled shrinkage

For Christina, from Scottsdale, Arizona, fitting into her designer jeans means she can relax.

Today I didn't need the scale to know I'd lost another 3 pounds. I used my shoes as the test. If I can sit on the edge of the bed, bend over, and tie my shoes without cutting off my breath, it means my gut is shrinking. It's such a relief to be able to breathe when I'm getting ready for work!

The top button on my pants is what put me on this diet. It was getting so I had to suck in just to get it fastened, and then I felt that pressure all day long. I refuse to buy a bigger size!

Well, this week I don't have to. I'm on the road and even feeling a bit lighter on my feet. Oh, I've been here before (can't quit eating desserts), but this time . . .

Breathing is a great motivator; we all want to keep doing it. Even if we don't get to the choking stage, it's a relief to feel comfortable in our clothes. And the extra energy that comes along with being lighter makes us look at those kids on the playground and think, "I could run if I really wanted to."

The accomplishment we feel when we meet our goal—10, 20, or 50 pounds later—boosts confidence in our looks and in our ability to control our own lives.

For women, the pressure to look good keeps diet gurus in fancy cars. Our weight gain is in our butts, which we can easily camouflage with longer jackets, hiding reality until it's shocking. Pregnantlike man-bellies are harder to disguise, so belt notches serve as constant reminders.

Feeling the gap in our pants—slipping more than one finger inside the waistband—is the green flag we've been hoping for. Relief is every day the gap widens.

Ultimate comfort: Maintaining goal weight

Loving Partners: Their caring makes you feel cherished

*Carole, from Medford, Oregon, thinks lovingly of
her man whenever she hears "our" songs.*

Today's my birthday and my husband made me breakfast. Those morning smells brought a joy I never feel
when I'm the one in the kitchen. I could hear bacon
cooking in the other room, but I didn't move. Doing
nothing is new for me; my days are always filled up with
lots of "shoulds." Mmmm, have you ever had a waffle
with a fresh-picked raspberry in every square and driz-
zled with homemade syrup? Well I have . . . now.

No dish cleanup for me. I just got up from the table
to the tune of clanking dishes and the cook telling me,
"I'm yours for the day, to do . . . whatever." Let's see,
since I'd been etching messages in the bathtub ring for
two weeks, that was next on the list. I could barely hear
the squirts of bathroom cleaner as I put on my newest
CD, sat squarely in front of the speakers, and listened to
love songs, which in my mind were about my man.

A matinee came next; my choice meant a comedy.
And even though he said it was so-so, I caught him laughing and secretly think he just doesn't want to admit there's
life beyond Clint.

Then it was home to rest up for an intimate celebration at a cozy French restaurant in town where a little wine, hand holding, and rack of lamb brought a glorious day to an end. Amazing how twelve short hours could make such a difference and erase the stress and boredom from living a life filled with details. And to think, some women are waiting for a valentine.

It doesn't matter *how* you know, only *that* you know. So many things say, "You matter." Everyone knows roses and chocolates mean a special occasion, but face it, they're gone in a day, have a zillion calories, and cost a small fortune. A look, a touch, or heartfelt notes, however, are all free.

Breakfast in bed or foot rubs or just plain listening—now that really says it. Sometimes love means doing nothing at all. Just leaving us alone when we need it means "I'm paying attention."

I know a tenderhearted husband who lies down beside his wife on the bed when she isn't feeling well. The cuddling, and his hand on her migraine head, always soothes and helps her to feel better.

Oh, it's great when partners celebrate their births with wine and candlelight, but it's those other, daily times that we remember most.

Massage: Body kneading at its finest

To Gail, from Sunnyvale, California, getting those rough spots worked is heaven.

Today I indulge, and spend a whole hour away from my life. There's just me and this person with very strong hands, who seems to know every muscle in my body and the attention it needs.

All my senses are pampered in that hour. With soft music in the background, each body part, taken one at a time, is ironed out until I'm a wet noodle. The sweet smell of almond oil, along with the muscle relaxation, all set the mood for an hour I want to visit again.

As I scoop my noodle off the table I know that here's a new name for my speed dial. Now all my essential contacts are a push button away: the doctor, mechanic, computer guy, *and* massage therapist.

Getting our bodies kneaded equals doggie belly rubbing. Just think about your dog and the look in her eyes when you scratch the top of her ears. She even asks for more by offering up her belly.

Getting a massage thirty years ago was reserved for la-ti-da health spas and Hollywood stars. Such an indulgence was unthinkable for everyday people, who always saved pampering for when they got sick or had a landmark birthday celebration, like forty.

Times have changed. Lifestyles these days are defined by constant activity, and our bodies demand a respite from the constant tension it brings. A massage gives us a breather. It does a body good.

Meditation: Stills a busy mind

Joey, from Grants Pass, Oregon, finds comfort in being peaceful inside.

I read a book about meditation once, never dreaming it was for average people like me. But today I hit the wall. Every morning my brain is jammed with a hundred different subjects, draining me before the day even begins. I'm tired of being tired.

I frantically searched for that book, reread the first chapter, and turned off the phone. Next I sat on the couch, took a deep breath, closed my eyes, and thought about my breaths, in/out, in/out. Calming my brain took awhile—random thoughts kept drifting in—but after 10 minutes, the noise in my head was gone. Breathing slower now. Brain unjammed.

Thoughts just keep on coming. Some float through unexpectedly, others squat for the long term and we can't shake them free no matter how hard we try. But there's hope; there's meditation.

A formal, Zenlike sit isn't necessary, with legs in impossible positions as we chant non-dictionary words. If we can schedule a pause in our day to sit still for 10 minutes, our monkey mind can hear intuition talking. Even the repetition of pulling weeds breaks the cycle of stress and causes it to lose momentum. A freer mind can then listen to gut feelings.

The trouble is, our parents never showed us how to slow down. They were too busy teaching us to do our best at all times. We grew up in families that valued accomplishments above all else—the kind you could touch, like first place or report card A's. It's why we're all striving to cram as much stuff as we can into every day.

People are proud of their busyness, wearing the word *busy* like a badge of honor. Witness the cell phone.

Meditation: Calming the noise in our heads

Lots of daily stress comes through our eyes. . . . Give them breaks.

Music: Mood maker

Bobbie, from Grants Pass, Oregon, listens to his favorite music—very loud—when he wants to break the stress.

I'm bored, bored, bored. Life has fallen back into a rut lately, and I need some sort of an uplift. When I'm in a funk like this, music always does the trick, flowing over my body like fairy dust, getting my life back on track.

Enter Elton. My own body shocks me. It's moving, and I'm powerless to stop the growing urge to sway. Some CDs just defy grumpy, and he's done it again, good old Dr. John.

Making my own

When you count the number of lessons I've had, you'd have to say I'm a lousy piano player. Two years of random lessons barely made a dent in my ability, but I figure my love of listening to music more than makes up for it. I couldn't afford lessons anymore so I quit, but I continue to practice and try to teach myself. It doesn't matter how good I play, just making the notes gives me pleasure. Even though structure gets mangled, you can still recognize the melodies.

To composers that are gone, I'd like to take this opportunity to apologize. I'm sure that Gershwin, Mozart, and

Lennon all turn over in their graves when I sit on my piano bench and try to be a part of their glory. To those who are still alive, I salute you, and please, know that I'm still trying.

M usic has power—to lift us up from humdrum, or slow us down from a busy day. The soft sounds of New Age calm all our senses, while the jarring bass of rock gets our juices flowing. Heavy metal, jazz, rap, and Mozart all set a mood and work their magic . . . whatever we need it to be.

Music = space filler. Remember those first empty minutes of a party you're hosting, when awkward guests who don't know each other search their brains for small talk? That silence makes you squirm. Music = icebreaker. Listening—voluntarily—to your teen's music narrows the generation gap. Music = movement. Where would aerobics be without it? And can you imagine a world without dance?

Music = memories, transporting us to another place, away from the inner demons of our past or the pace of freeway driving. It brings back the past . . . of high school glory days or a smile from someone special. Where would the world of romance be without Our Songs?

It gives us courage and is why we use the phrase "whistling in the dark." Making noise lets us pretend we're not alone.

Maybe it's why the slaves sang in the fields; they needed courage. Music gave them company, but also lifted their spirits to help them get through each day.

Making our own music lets us feel like part of the process. We get to go beyond just listening or dancing or singing and produce the sound that we love . . . or nearly. We get to double our pleasure.

Parents may not have this in mind when they turn into lesson Nazis. They want us constantly to live up to our potential and yearn to brag about our accomplishments to their friends. Who knows, maybe there's an untapped Mozart in some of us at eight, but more likely it's just payback time; their parents did it to them. In the end we thank our parents— silently, of course—for depriving us of baseball time, because now we can read a note or two.

Played too loud, music is a barrier to conversation, but also fills the space if you don't want any. Don't call a therapist or pour a stiff one, just play a CD.

Music: A mood maker, a body shaker

Naps: Day breaks

Carol, from Grants Pass, Oregon, rejuvenates in the middle of the day.

I closed my eyes for an instant at 3:00 P.M., this time on my bed and under the covers. Forty-five minutes later I woke up from a dream, which is something I didn't know I could have in the middle of the day. My eyes snapped open, and I realized that this had been even better than a full night's sleep. I felt like a new person.

By the time I walked into the kitchen, ideas were zinging around, bouncing off the inside walls of my skull. I suddenly knew what I had to do and when I had to do it. Just-right phrases for my book suddenly appeared, along with two appointments I had forgotten to write on the calendar. I even had the energy to cook a decent meal. This was big.

Today's nap-miracle cleared months of cobwebs from my brain, giving me renewed perspective and the power to concentrate . . . if only until bedtime.

Mostly naps are for old folks. It's what our grandpa does when his rocking chair tires him out, right? Wrong.

Naps are fine, anytime. We just don't know it when we're twenty-nine, when staying up until 2:00 A.M. and then getting up at 6:00 for work doesn't faze us much. By the time ten years pass—and those morning-afters get tougher—we begin to realize that Grandpa is very smart. Naps catch us up when our brains won't settle down for hours the night before.

The luxury of napping, or even pausing, on a workday is a seldom-recognized perk of getting older and retiring. Instead of cursing the passing years, we can celebrate the catching up we get to do—of sleep, of pondering, of listening more than we used to.

Achievement and money rule in American culture, so pausing on purpose seems downright rude. But just think how much better we'd work, how much more productive we'd be, if we adopted a little siesta culture. What if mothers napped along with their young children instead of catching up on housework? Those rearing years would be easier to get through. Even a 10-minute lie-down relieves scratchy eyes and a sagging spirit.

Nature: Comfort #1

Kathy, from Selma, Oregon, connects with nature by riding her bike along the river to look for the first signs of spring.

Here I am in the woods, free from city sounds . . . alone, silent, watching, listening. Only the sound of the fountain beside me breaks the silence. The soft splashing starts attracting birds, and the bliss of my break is complete, but wait . . . here comes a doe. She doesn't notice me—I'm very still and not wearing red today—as she strolls 6 feet from my chair, leading her twin Bambis. This must be a dream. Her fawns are smaller than my Lab. Trotting unsteadily, they stick very close to Mom, who stops periodically and patiently waits as they suckle their morning snack. By now I'm hoping they can't hear me smiling, because the slightest noise will end it all.

Eventually I have to move. Their appearance catches me off guard, and I've played statue longer than I ever did in second grade. Turning my head sends them scattering. These new little creatures have already learned to run, with cute little mini-bounds, *bam bam bam.*

Connecting with nature was the # 1 comfort in my survey—listening to it, watching it, walking through it, or playing in it. Some of us strive to harmonize; others merely use her for convenience. Maybe it's the color; they say green is soothing. Maybe it's knowing that the squirrels accept us just the way we are. Or maybe we think animals have it made. After all, compared to our lives and our busy brains, animals only have two things to think about—eating and being eaten. It's an awesome dilemma, true, but the simplicity of it all is compelling.

We all relate to nature in our own way, whether it's biking along a river path, kicking a pile of autumn leaves, or watering the spider plant on our desk at work. Gardeners wait for their favorite bulbs to peek through in the spring because daffodils bring relief from gray days. And if we want to feel her power, we can head for the beach in the winter to feel the rage of a storm.

We can study nature, make love in it, and we can eat it. There are times, however, when it's just plain annoying. The thunder of the surf can mean earplugs at bedtime. And the soothing coo of mourning doves isn't, after three constant hours. The itch of poison oak, a drilling tick, or a nasty sunburn can give doubts, but in the end, nature has what we're all looking for—a respite from everything.

Nature: There must be something to it—
birds are never in a bad mood.

Camel hairbrushes are made of squirrel's hair.

Old Hats (and New): Cap off a great mood

Betty, from Grants Pass, Oregon, discovered that her grandmother's advice works: "Buy a hat when you feel low."

I have a soft hat for every occasion. Most of them are hanging on nails in the garage so every day I can pick the one that fits the mood I'm in.

My favorite is the one I look way cool in. It's red, soft, and well worn, with a bill that has just the right curve to it. It has a patch with wings and the number 032 on the front, but I can't remember where I got it, or what that's about. To me it means, "Oh, I wish I owned a '32 Ford."

My blue and gold striped visor is for going to the beach or boating. It has the word *Epcot* on it and reminds me of my trip to Florida. Next to that are three sweaty stinkies that I rotate when I'm working or exercising. These just keep the sun out of my eyes and have different company names on them.

The one hat that still looks new after five years is the one I hardly ever wear. It hangs on my bedpost next to an underwater photograph of tropical fish and has my old scuba diving patch sewn on it. The color of the patch matches the color of the water in the picture. Seeing it hanging there every night when I go to bed reminds me of when I swam with these very same fish twenty years ago.

On golf days I have three hats to pick from, all green in different stages of wear. On vacation trips I visit local pro shops and pick ones I like with the club's insignia on them.

The bottom nail is reserved for those days when I'm in an ugly mood. And even though that torn, stained, worn-out gray hat is my least favorite, it's still warm and comfy on my head.

An old hat is as comfy as an old pair of shoes, which get softer and softer with each wearing. The more it's handled—the more action it sees—the more it becomes like an old friend, waiting its turn for headspace.

A balding head seeks camouflage, squinting eyes seek shade, and, of course, baseball demands a logo. But practical isn't the point; image and mood are defined by a hat lover's pick of the day. When people pass him on the street and look at his hat, that day's pick could be conversational, but also controversial. Either way, selection determines connection.

Dilemma: An ugly-mood hat pick versus the cool look we need to impress a new girlfriend

You can only put ¾ gallon into a 10-gallon hat.

Orion and Family: Sky glitter starts a party in your heart

Linda, from Grants Pass, Oregon, feels a sense of peace and appreciation for the awesome number of stars above her at night.

Instead of renting a movie last night, we took a blanket to the backyard and lay head to head on our backs for an hour of sky watching.

It's been fifteen years since my last science class, so the Big Dipper is the only name I know, but that didn't matter. All that mattered was dark and stars. The night sky reminded me of the black canvas of a Lite Brite toy after my niece had poked pegs through it.

My boyfriend tried to impress me with space facts by pointing out constellations, but I was happy just gazing. Any problems I had before diminished in that hour to specks smaller than those I saw in front of me.

In grammar school we learn what this nighttime sky glitter really is—balls of fire far away. But since we can't even imagine the magnitude of it all, we store it in that part of our brains reserved for magic and ESP and the X-files.

Astronomers, whose telescopes confirm another world, know that what's happening is not sleight of hand. And to those of us who did just enough homework to recognize the vastness, star watching is all about awe. To the rest of us, stars are merely reliable; they're always there, and always the same. We know they don't go away, but just hide behind the clouds, waiting to come out so they can predict a clear day tomorrow.

Why stars are linked to romance isn't a mystery. It's always been a good excuse to park on some out-of-the-way street, where gazing sometimes turns to groping. Stars provide good cover for a breakup—his planet is lapping over the wrong cusp of her planet at the wrong time. The night sky is a good excuse for kids to stay up past bedtime—"A comet's coming at midnight." Lying outside on the grass after dark is breaking lots of rules, so it feels more like a party than science discovery.

In the end, maybe what makes us smile is simply the twinkles, reminding us of good times under Christmas lights.

The trouble with stars: They happen while we're asleep.

People created constellations to make sense of the sky. A star chart helps you find Orion the Hunter. He holds up his shield and club against Taurus the Bull, a nearby constellation, who appears ready to charge. A line of three bright stars makes up Orion's belt.

Peaceful People: Calm is contagious

Carol, from Grants Pass, Oregon, feels very comfortable around soft voices and calm souls.

The hectic pace of my days and the constant noise in my head are like a merry-go-round that never stops to let me off. Luckily, there's a pause once in a while. Those are on the days when I get to see my friend Diane. She doesn't know yet what she does for me — a new perspective when I need it most, like today.

The trouble is I try too hard, always striving to do every little thing perfectly. After a while I notice how tight my shoulders are, and that I have an angry look on my face. I'm not mad, just concentrating. I start talking faster and faster, and get crankier and crankier.

Luckily, today is a Diane Day. Her soft, sincere voice always calms me down. In walked my angel, with her calm-o-meter registering 10. The static in my head slowed down, and suddenly I felt like stopping to take a deep breath. Getting through the day was much easier after that.

Some people have a special look, a face that has the ability to calm us. We connect right away—not in a lover sense or even a friendship sense, but just for that moment. It's all about the eyes . . . and lingering. Peaceful souls never rush off. They want to relish every moment, so they never plan appointments back-to-back. As life swirls around them, they appear to be moving in slow motion. They are the eye of many peoples' storms.

We recognize them immediately when their eyes don't move on and their mouths don't chatter. They're looking us in the eyes, listening, and we're sure they understand just what we're going through. With a voice and a face that's softer than most, their smiles are always welcoming. People who've achieved an inner calm have the power to bring us down from the mania of constant motion.

Photos: Passports to memories

Chris, from El Dorado Hills, California, was always comforted by her photographs and shared memories.

Tonight I wanted to remember, to go back to a different time. I hadn't anticipated so many smiles, but every page of my photo album started a vivid recollection of little stories. I was surprised by how many things I've done over the years, and how easy it was to relive the events. Was it really that long ago that we got our first new car? I remember that dark green Mustang like it was yesterday. Boy, I wish I still had it.

I returned to some pages again and again, like the all-day beach parties or the excitement of a new baby in our home. I was so anxious, and wondered how such a little thing could scare me so much. My constant question was, "What do I do now?"

It felt weird to flip through the pages of my life in two hours, but taking time out once in a while to reflect on the good times keeps me from forgetting. And reminds me — again — to count my blessings.

Getting stuck in "remembering when" is easy, especially when then was better than now. Even if looking back means occasional tears, there's always at least one photo to cherish. Remembering when things were different from now is like renting a movie of the younger you: the vacations, baby's first step, the old make-out car, or the sweat it took to plant your first lawn.

Where would traveling businessmen, GIs, and kids away from home be without someone they love to carry in their pocket? Sometimes it's all they have when being alone isn't good anymore. And have you ever noticed how some children never age? You're thirty-five, but your dad's wallet, and everyone who looks at it, thinks you're five. Is this because you were cuter then, or did he forget you grew up?

Professional photographers, who capture weddings, portraits, and great shots on the basketball court, make fortunes. But it's still the candid, headless pictures that provide laughter and great memories for us all.

Every family has a designated picture taker, the one who's mostly missing from the album. While some of them are dedicated to lining everyone up to grin, others are strictly stealth shooters. With a tiny camera hidden in their pocket, they can snap a shot before anyone notices. And surprise appearances in their videos provide lots of laughs and embarrassing moments.

Snapshotting: Head lopping—a.k.a.
imperfection—makes it better.

Whatever you do, *hold your camera steady*. Forget those chicken wings; get your arms down and brace them against your body. Hold your breath or use a tripod.

—Phil Watkins at Photo Den, Grants Pass, Oregon

Playing: A break from everydayness

Suzi, from Rogue River, Oregon, gets great joy
by playing with her daughter, a.k.a. her dog.

Emily knows how to play tag, and it's what we do together every weekend. Emily's my Lab and my child and the smartest dog in the world. She's really a human in disguise. My friends laugh when I say that, but if you could only see the way she looks at me. I know she knows what I'm thinking.

When I assume the time-for-tag stance — half-crouched, knees bent, feet apart, looking her in the eye — we square off and take off, trying to catch each other around trees and bushes, or any obstacle in the backyard. Laughing is impossible not to do. Emily smiles, you know.

Playing give us an excuse to relax and let our hair down. Getting a break from daily rituals gives us a breather and a chance to start fresh. Whole days are best, but play moments are easier to arrange. Take a minute to wrestle with the dog. Steal an hour and bike to a playground and swing. Plan a day at the beach and let the waves chase your toes. Any diversion counts.

We seldom hear the word *play* when we talk about grown-ups; children play, adults enjoy recreation. People whisper in disgust, "When will she ever grow up?" when they see us having too much fun, or buying dinner at a restaurant too often instead of cooking our own. But that's the whole point; ignoring responsibility defines play.

On play: Watch the children. Imitate them.

Prayer: Help is on the way

Jan, from Grants Pass, Oregon, finds great comfort in her faith.

"How are we going to make it? Oh dear God, please help me." It's a question I ask a lot lately. The fact is I skipped dinner last night so the kids could eat, and now I'm staring down at the third and final notice from the power company. This minimum-wage job just isn't getting it, and I'm scared every day that one of us will get sick and need a doctor.

Last year I thought starting over had to be better than living with him another day. The drinking and the never-ending criticism and put-downs were more than I could live with. And then I began to notice how nervous the kids were just before their dad got home. So we left him, the town, and the grief behind. But I didn't think it would be so hard to make ends meet.

Ten months have passed now in my new town, and once again I was dreading the mailman. He only brings bills I can't pay. But wait. This time there was an envelope from the IRS with something green showing through the window. I knew what that meant—a government check. I'd forgotten all about my tax refund.

"Thank you, thank you, thank you for this gift, just when I needed it most." I guess it wasn't more than I could handle, after all.

P rayer is like setting a balloon free in the wind; you release your worries by handing them over to a power that knows the ropes, or rather, the strings. You've been going in circles trying to come up with a solution, so letting it go lightens the load.

Some of us are private pray-ers, reciting our rosary rote or just plain talking—in regular everyday language. To us it's just an ordinary conversation with a close friend. You know you can tell this friend anything, and he will understand and not think you're silly or stupid or crazy. And because miracles have happened just when we needed them most, we know someone, or something, is looking after us. We're never alone. Best of all, here's someone who believes in us when even *we* don't.

Some of us are public pray-ers, congregating in churches and for vigils and revivals. We're sure God is with us in church because it's a building specifically designated for our time with him. He can hear us better there than at home, so we sing his praises, remind him of how much we're thinking about him, and give thanks for what he blessed us with the week before. If the power of prayer swells with numbers, the voices that sing and pray as one can't help but get heavenly attention.

The fact that we set aside this time to get out of our grubbies and concentrate on God sets church apart as our haven from everyday living. We know we're safe here. And if we move to a new town, the congregation welcomes us and gives us new friends so we don't feel so isolated.

Prayer: Gives you hope that help is on the way

Thank you.

Quiet: When you can hear your own eyes blink

Sue, from Merlin, Oregon, seeks the serenity of total silence . . . except for trickling and tweeting.

I didn't know what quiet was before. I'm forty-five and up until now thought quiet was the middle of the night when the noise from traffic, car alarms, and phones faded. Today I went above the birds—something I didn't know you could do—and found out what silence really was.

We drove out of town for about an hour, parked the car, and then hiked for another hour. The sounds of civilization faded as the ground got steeper. At first it was enough to leave the constant hum of the highway. But after that was gone, and I got used to hearing nothing but the sound of our own footsteps, even the birds seemed loud. We hiked higher and higher, and then heard it— nothing. Nothing but dead silence. I could actually look down on flying birds, and when you're above them you can't hear them.

It was eerie at first, but heaven afterward. I sat down on a boulder by the edge of the path for half an hour before I dared speak. It felt like breaking the silence would be against the law here.

Three sure ways to escape noise: deep in the woods, on top of a mountain, on the golf course. So that's why the game is so popular.

Total silence is rare unless you live in big country like Montana, where you can hear the squirrels chew. Listening to the rustle of trees or the whir of a hummer's wings is foreign to those of us who live in LA or New York City. Our peace comes only when factories and traffic slow their pace at night, or jack hammerers pause for lunch. When we finally find it on the weekend, the silence makes us want to whisper, as if daring to break it will alert some librarian someplace to shush us.

Young families with small children seldom experience silence, while seniors sometimes have too much . . . and quiet turns into lonely. References to silence are old: "You could hear a pin drop," "He was quiet as a mouse," "Silence is golden." And the phrase "dead silence" is obvious every time we thread our way through the headstones in an ancient graveyard.

Maybe the reason people move when they retire, or why retirement communities are so quiet, is that after fifty years of noisy living their brains insist on a break. Imagine the quiet quest of workers who have had loud machinery in their ears for thirty years. Noise to them is like a battering ram on their brains, flooding their minds with constant aggravation. When they finally do achieve it, silence seeps in like the warmth of the sun.

It's easy to become a quiet-addict, when even the hum of your own refrigerator is aggravating.

Hearing loss is the most common irreversible occupational hazard in the world. More than 30 million Americans are exposed to hazardous sound levels on a regular basis at work, home, and play.

- Classroom background noise: 20–30 dB
- Refrigerator hum: 40 dB
- Conversation: 60–70 dB
- City traffic: 80 dB
- Prolonged exposure that results in permanent loss: 90 dB
- Motorcycle, firecrackers, small firearms: 120–140 dB
- Threshold of pain: 130 dB

Reading: Adventure in your lap

Shauna, from Fort Riley, Kansas, likes to curl up with a good book and a cup of hot tea.

Wow, the hard copy. I've been buying paperbacks for so many years that I forgot what a real book feels like. Waiting for the second printing into paperback was never a choice I liked; it was a budget requirement.

You wouldn't think you could actually fondle a book, but the cover was so smooth I couldn't resist. Besides, it felt good just sitting in my lap. After dinner I had a little ceremony in my head—a little drum roll—as I sat in the living room and cracked it open for the first time.

My bookcase is filled with paperbacks, but this one is going to sit on the shelf reserved for hard covers. . . . Only six are there so far. And definitely, no lending out; that would mean losing it for sure.

Books transport us. We don't need money to travel, a classroom to learn, or the guts to jump out of a plane because it's all there, right in our lap. Nonfiction feeds our curiosity, fiction provides escape, and inspirationals give us courage to change.

Have you ever read a book that really spoke to you, as if the author must know you? These titles always call to us when we're browsing. Some of us love our books so much that we dare not open them too far for fear of creasing the cover or cracking the spine. But tattered books always seem more interesting, as if they've given lots of pleasure over the years. Kind of like a crowded restaurant; you just figure it must be good.

Sharing the joy of reading connects us with our children, whether we read to them or listen patiently while they read to us. Taking turns creating different endings adds to the fun and gives laptime an extra boost.

Books are everywhere, for everyone. You can pay 25¢ for a tattered paperback at a yard sale, $75 for an art book at Borders, or hang out at the library. Even if you can't read, there are books on tape. If you can't see, there's Braille.

You never catch a real reader without a book. They carry one everywhere, just in case they have a free minute during the day. I once had a friend who read labels while she sat on the pot. If you're a true reader, she told me, you read everything in sight, even toilet paper wrapping. And although some neatniks see books as clutter, or maybe a good doorstop, diehards can't wait to hang out in the bookstore or to crack open a new one.

Schedules: Planning ahead gives you something to look forward to

Don, from Concord, California, depends on having something to look forward to every week.

I look forward to Tuesdays, the day I go out to lunch and get fussed over. My favorite waitress, Alice, has been serving me lunch for seventeen years now, so if it's crowded I just wait until there's a table open in her station.

Maria's was our favorite restaurant when my wife was alive, but now I depend on my Tuesday lunches for the company and relief from staring into an empty refrigerator. I'm not too good at cooking for myself yet. Alice has become an old friend, and when I don't show on my regular day, she drops by the house to check up on me.

On the other days of the week, I get to see my children. They live close by and always call to make sure I'm doing OK. I used to race my cruiser, but these days I'm too unsteady and don't see well enough to go by myself, so once a month my daughter and I spend the day together cruising through the delta. Once a week my son cooks me breakfast. When I wake up Sundays at six, he's already in the kitchen making my favorite, corned beef hash. I love that hour we have together every week.

These are the times I look forward to now. These are the times I can count on.

If we have plenty of time on our hands, scheduling a lunch date next Tuesday is something we look forward to the whole week. It's especially true for seniors, who sometimes have nothing but time. Days seem longer than before when we're eighty-five and living alone; a lot of our friends are gone by now, and our children are busy with their own lives.

A more familiar tune is "never having enough" time in the day, so we plan our hours, or half-hours, to make sure everything gets done. Setting daily goals gives the illusion that we're moving forward, and it's comforting to know we're not standing still.

We can set our clocks by some schedulers. The ones who order Chinese take-out every Wednesday night, no matter what comes up, boost scheduling to its finest hour. On the other hand, if you call a friend in the morning to invite him over at five o'clock and he replies, "How do I know what I'll want to do by five?" you know—here's a man who knows how to relax. For those of us who yearn to slow down, *this* is scheduling at its finest.

Best schedule of all: Vacation itinerary

Shopping: Happiness is bargain hunting

Craig, from Tracy, California, loves to cut a deal, like spending money on a bargain.

Shopping won the debate in my head this time. I thought about going to a movie, but theaters are always filled with couples, and I feel weird there alone.

It's Friday and I got off work early. Wearing the skirt to work that I want to buy a top for saved me from driving home and coming back. I was headed for the mall by two minutes after two.

Starting off with a treat is very important—it's my personal mall etiquette—so I stopped at the food court for a cinnamon twist. It's also important that you pick something you can eat while you walk around. That way you don't waste any time.

After five stores and trying on nine blouses, I finally found one that matched the teal stripe in my skirt. And since I don't get here very often, I picked up a tan scarf with a teal swirl running through it (40 percent off), two pairs of pantyhose, and a new pair of earrings that I didn't need. Earrings are my weakness, especially gold hoops.

By the time I got home, I was totally high on my "finds."

Shopping is a tribute to our hunter-gatherer legacy. And the mall is a tribute to our shopping obsession. As credit card receipts are signed, shoppers gather purchases, stuffing one bag into a larger one when the number of packages gets too awkward to carry. Hunger instinct has been satisfied . . . until the next time. Contentment is evident as smiling, focused faces pass each other between stores—gathering, gathering, gathering.

Having birthday money in our wallet eases the guilt that women, teenagers, and the occasional man have from constantly confusing their wants with their needs. Shopping relieves the cabin fever that stay-at-home moms, full-time homemakers, and seniors often get; stores automatically mean people, and this marks the end to a lonely day.

Owning stuff makes us feel richer than we are, and no matter if it's retail. Uncovering a gem in a thrift store is actually double the pleasure because pickin's are slimmer. Finding the right combo of color, style, and size is tough. But when we do, satisfaction of the hunt is complete.

Smiles: Give you a natural high

Kim, from Grants Pass, Oregon, smiles at people for no reason at all.

The decision about whether I'd go to the party had taken a week—yes, no, yes, no, yes, no. I wasn't sure that I could face another room full of strangers. Those first few minutes are always so agonizing that 15 minutes seem like an hour.

I decided to go at the last minute, but after I got there started to fidget after a minute or two. Then something across the room gave me hope—a smile pointed my way. The room suddenly seemed friendlier, and my face relaxed enough to smile back. That simple grin got me beyond the goofy comments I sometimes make when I'm nervous.

A smile says, "Welcome." A smile says, "You matter." In a room full of strangers it diminishes that awkward, self-conscious feeling of being alone.

A simple smile coming our way softens whatever mood we're in, just like the first sunny days in March warm the winter earth. It's easy to misinterpret the warmth of a sales pitch as the real thing because that smile connection is a warm fuzzy we all crave.

A smile: "How you doin'?" without words

Sounds: Just listen

Jean, from Grants Pass, Oregon, can't help smiling when she hears that the 49ers won their game.

Out of the blue came a sound from my youth, probably everybody's youth. I took a walk tonight because it was so quiet outside, and the hot day had finally cooled down. The sound of a music box halfway down the block caught my ear, and it took a minute to realize what it was—the ice-cream truck. Images of a younger me popped into my head, of the whole family scrambling for loose change when they heard "the man" turn the corner to our block, and of six little faces surrounding the ice-cream guy, yelling their favorites all at once. Fudgsicle was always mine. I'd forgotten all about that sound. Too busy being a grown-up, I guess.

A sound from our youth instantly transports us to a time when *responsibility* was just a word our parents used a lot. They said we needed to get more of it. Hearing music from the past recalls first loves, first dances, and happily bugging parents with our kind of music.

Most of us agree to love soft rain on the roof, songbirds, and laughter. And just about everyone agrees about fingernails on the blackboard. But some sounds are up for grabs. The thunder of a healthy hot rod is soothing only to an engine lover, and the sound of a dog barking an "intruder alert" is music to its owner's ears.

White noise machines: Replacing one
annoyance with another

A good game

I sit very still—outside—and close my eyes.

Listening is easier that way.

The number of different sounds just multiplied.

Sun: Lifts sagging spirits

Joanne, from Los Altos, California, sits in the sunshine until she feels mellow.

I took a break today from working—and thinking—to sit on the porch and let the sun bury my face. It's April and the sun was a welcome relief from gray days. As I sat pointing my face upward, my brain paused. Maybe it's celebrating the warmth, or maybe it's just tired of gray and the daily grind.

All it took was 15 minutes. I felt refreshed, as if I could go back to work and begin again.

By April, the gray and gloom since November have left a gaping hole in our mood. It's why that first sunny day calls everyone outside. Suddenly there are more smiles, more flowers, and more giggling children.

Plants and people both perk up with long-awaited blue skies. The sun brings out the best of Earth with new buds everywhere and daffodils reminding us to start thinking about our garden. Boaters have been waiting since last fall to launch, and the scent of barbequing burgers drifts through every suburban neighborhood. People emerge, planting pansies or just walking around the block.

Now, before going outside, they think about lotions— against sunburn, mosquitoes, and dry air. Teenagers are worried about freckles while their mothers notice age spots, wrinkles, or worse.

The sun: Nature's antidepressant

Support: Backup means you're not alone

Dianna, from San Jose, California, just has to remember that her family and friends are always there for her.

My wife saved me last year. Her words of encouragement convinced me to quit working after forty long years. The relief is incredible.

It never dawned on me to just quit. I'd been the breadwinner for so long that to me there was no choice until Social Security. I'd been gritting my teeth for almost five years and secretly counting down, looking forward to every birthday that brought it closer. For the first time in my life, getting older was a good thing.

I'd planned to muddle through until sixty-two, and was surprised by how calm she was when she suggested I retire now. I had always thought that women worried a lot about money and security. She told me that being miserable every day would make me sick, and that my health was the most important thing. That's all it took. Freedom was in sight.

Imagine me being more important to her than money! My heart is full, and my smile is constant. These days I catch myself whistling . . . for no particular reason.

Just knowing someone's in our corner reduces pressure; we know for sure we have a safety net and that someone really cares what happens to us.

If life suddenly slips, our "net" doesn't lecture; they just show up with a box of Kleenex. We can count on them for encouraging words about our wacky idea or a few bucks in a pinch, and their clear head takes the panic out of a crisis. Sometimes the extra boost even gives us courage to tiptoe into new and scary places.

Some of us boast about not needing anyone. We're proud of being self-sufficient in every way and wouldn't dare ask for help—even if it means a hernia from lifting a refrigerator by ourselves, or cruising around San Francisco aimlessly until a familiar landmark looms. But under that crust of competence, even these stubborn souls secretly yearn for warm words.

Moral support: Truss for the soul

Talk: Getting it out

*Alice, from Grants Pass, Oregon, finds pleasure
in good conversation over a great meal.*

Every Saturday morning my husband and I gravitate to
what we've dubbed our "communication station"—the
place we always sit to talk. It's on the couch, facing the
large window overlooking the bird feeders. That first cup
of coffee always gets some discussion started; it's warm,
smells great, and having something to do with our hands
acts as a buffer when we start to get fidgety with the words.
This is the place where decisions are made, feelings are
aired, and fears diminish. This is where my mind gets
lighter, while the intimacy grows between us.

Nothing takes the pressure off as fast as talking; mouths
are like pressure valves that need to be cracked open
once in a while. Stress accumulates behind them like
balloons left on the helium valve too long. It doesn't have to
be a long conversation, and it doesn't have to be with anyone
else but you. Another perspective, however, helps iron out the
day faster. Some of us talk way too much, with a constant
stream of blibber-blabber that repels even the consummate

listener. Others don't speak up enough, and end up being everyone's doormat.

Stay-at-home moms with small children yearn to talk to someone who can talk back and understands what they're saying. (Being with young people is wonderful, but not all the time.) These moms can be seen standing on the street, waiting for the mailman; sometimes any warm body will do.

Having yourself to talk to is very handy—you're always so available to you. Granted, sometimes you're too busy to listen, but intuition always gives pretty good advice. And even though it's hard to escape scoldings, debates are always civilized—no yelling or chair throwing or hurt feelings. In fact, great insights come from the little courtroom in your head, after both sides argue it out.

Communication: The key to avoiding a meltdown

Taste: Comfort begins with a bite

Joe, from Talent, Oregon, looks forward to Slurpees—
a treat that takes him back to his childhood.

In the early weeks of our marriage we had a small apartment in a new town. I hadn't looked for a job yet, so cooking, cleaning, and waiting for my honey to come home from work every day was all I did for a while. Being together seemed all that was important then. Staying in, of course, was our newlywed habit.

One of our highlights of the week was the small party we planned with each other on Sunday afternoons. The only snack I knew how to make at the time was onion dip. The layout was simple—a bag of ruffles, small bowl of dip, and two tall glasses of Coke.

To get our taste buds primed, we skipped lunch so we would be good and hungry. I can still remember that first scoop. After that, the race was on. The feverish dipping, and the fact that my new husband was dipping three chips at a time, forced us to revert to playground rules—taking turns. Dipping rules were now established. Did you know that when the dip is low, and the chips are too small to hold, you can dump the scraps into the dip bowl and eat them with a spoon? This was a trick I'd never seen before—Mom and Dad had always politely dipped one chip at a time. They did everything politely.

There was no need to wash the bowl because my own trick was to run a finger around the bowl when only traces were left. You see the need for party rules.

We still laugh about our cheap thrills—ten years later.

Whatever your pleasure—fresh veggies from the garden, hot chocolate by the fireplace, or chip and dip—food and drink are high on everyone's comfort list. And favorites are predictable. Taste buds seldom crave liver or Brussels sprouts, more like ice cream, chocolate, potato chips, and even red Popsicles.

Our lives revolve around food. We consume it, and are consumed by it. We talk about it, buy it, fix it, and eat it. What's defined as only one of our senses—taste—really engages all of them. The smell of cookies in the oven prepares our taste buds for what's ahead, and our eyes feast on the plate presentation of a gourmet chef. A fine meal not only tranquilizes the crabby mood of an empty stomach but signals the unconscious remnants of our ancestors that we've survived one more day.

In fact, most of our social contacts are built around meals, cocktails, or late-night desserts. Where would we go on first dates if it weren't for restaurants, where eating gives us something to do with our hands during awkward conversation gaps? What else would children throw on wild days in the cafeteria? And women's magazines would have to find a new obsession if it weren't for diet plans.

Pressure starts early; Mom always made us eat when we didn't want to. She made us eat stuff we didn't like, and gave us treats to keep us quiet. No wonder we're out of whack about food.

Eating and drinking: Oral therapy

The reason foods lose their flavor when we have a cold is because our sense of flavor is affected by how things smell. Also, food must be moist or contain fats to be tasted.

Touch: Body-to-body keeps you connected

To Adrienne, from Henderson, Nevada,
comfort comes not only from being touched,
but also by touching.

I wake up too early, and it's still too dark and too cold to get out of bed. I make a secret little sound or "accidentally" roll over too close and like magic, we're both awake. We turn onto our sides, both facing the same way. Then we draw our knees up and slide closer to make two spoons cupped together. These moments are always silent—talking interrupts the mood. After a while we turn and face the other way, keeping the spoons in tact as we turn, rolling over as one. This intimate ritual sets a tone for the whole day. It starts us smiling.

wo bodies nestling in bed fit snuggly together like two puzzle pieces. And doing it in that drowsy space, just after we open our eyes in the morning, is touching at its finest. The touch of a lover reminds us how much we're cherished. And when we fight, a simple pat means it's over; touching when we're still mad just doesn't feel right.

Skin-to-skin with a lover on a cold night substitutes for flannel nightgowns and hot water bottles, but just the warm arms of a friend calm us down and says, "I'm with you." Hugs that linger smooth and soothe us. Just sitting right next to someone we care for—shoulder to shoulder—connects that sense of togetherness.

A mystery: Why do we excuse ourselves for standing too close or walking in front of someone at the grocery store? We apologize for just stepping into the space surrounding them. Our culture's taboo on touching, especially between men, makes us weary and frightened to reach out to children and other adults. So we make up for it by the empty hugs that substitute for hand shakes. These fake hugs subtract from their worth by turning into a mere courtesy. Maybe we should all take a cue from the monkeys at the zoo, who divide their time between eating, sleeping, and picking fleas out of each other's fur.

Unclutter: Strive to KIS (Keep It Simple)

For Rich, from Portland, Oregon, clearing the decks for what's next calms his mind.

I thought I might have an ulcer. Then I started to notice how much better I felt on vacations. In fact, every short trip away from the house was the same; I really felt better away from it. Then one day it clicked—maybe it was my house that was making me sick. Ever since my second child was born, my small house was literally growing clutter, and I never, ever had the time to organize anything or to throw anything away. Sometimes it seems like the clutter's alive and moving inward, maybe even multiplying. And I can never find anything when I need it.

After talking for months about how lousy I felt all the time, a friend took pity on me yesterday. She said I needed a push to get started, so she came over to help. We tackled the bookcase first; it's in the center of the living room and the shelves looked like we had stood back and thrown things in from across the room. Everything was every which way.

We emptied it out, and then sat on the floor vacuuming the top of every book, picture frame, video, and miscellaneous junk. Then the hard part—putting back only the things I needed. Movies went to the top shelf, textbooks on the left side, fiction on the right, photos down to eye level, and my son's books on the bottom. Health books, cookbooks, magazines, travel, inspirational—my God, no wonder I can't find anything. Clearing these shelves—we filled three cardboard boxes with donations, returns, and trash—was like a treasure hunt. There was an overdue book from the library, a book a friend loaned me more than a year ago, and three missing puzzle pieces that hung us up last Christmas.

I slept great last night, and this morning got up and walked to the kitchen past my brand "new" bookcase. The tone of the whole house changed overnight. My stomachache is gone. There's hope at last.

Feng shui-ers tell us to unclutter ourselves because having too much stuff stops the free flow of energy around us and through our homes. They say it changes lives by bringing fortune, starting relationships, improving health.

Scoffers, who don't like fancy words, call it a crock. But let's face it, too much clutter in our face diverts; our vision is dispersed around too many objects. Think of Wal-Mart, where every inch is filled with merchandise, and then think of an art gallery, where empty rooms display just a handful of paintings. Somewhere in between is a good formula for our homes.

Clear space helps us focus on what's really important, not the doodads surrounding us. Just trying to find something buried under the rubble is reason enough to start sorting. It's a fact of life—accumulating is what we do best. More is better; TV and magazines tell us so. Bucking this trend isn't easy, but starting in one room, or one drawer or bookcase, is a good experiment.

Think of how each piece of stuff multiplies after it's home. We then have to: find a place for it, dust it, trip over it, repair it, get rid of its replacement, worry about burglars, store it when we're tired of it, wait for people who never show when we try to sell it.

On clutter: Chaos begets chaos,
in our homes, and in our minds.

To get started, label five cardboard boxes:

- Garbage
- Fix-it
- Recycle
- Relocate
- Can't decide: Hide this box for a month. Then before you open it, try to remember what's inside. If you can't, life has continued without them. So . . .

—Adapted from *Clear the Clutter with Feng Shui* by Karen Kingston

Understanding Ears: Hear how you feel

To Kathy, from Grants Pass, Oregon, finding someone who's "really" listening is rare . . . but glorious.

The idea of a support group to me had always meant a bunch of whiners sitting in a circle spilling their guts to one another. Who needs that? Well, after three years of constantly struggling to put on a happy face, I'm beginning to think I do. My depression must have been showing lately, because my son started to badger me. He said joining a group would help.

I finally gave in, but he had to drive, and then drag me to the door. Surprise, surprise. They didn't laugh at me and my whining. In fact, the room was filled with clones of me. They understood. When I think about all those years I hid my real feelings about everything, I could cry. And I have.

t takes courage to 'fess up . . . to unload and confess. We think people will judge us or hate us for how weird we are. But getting it out fosters an inner calm. Finding that special someone, who really hears what we're saying, is the hard part. When we finally do, that listening ear can unlock years of fears, or cheer us up when it's just the blues for a day. It doesn't even have to be out loud; a simple nod means they're listening and understand what we're going through.

Confiding in friends and lovers is what most of us do, but sometimes strangers pour their hearts out. Strangers are safe. We're not afraid of their judgment because, in our own mind, it doesn't matter what they think. They are there for just that moment . . . or so we hope.

The relief when secrets are finally out changes lives, like shedding a 40-pound pack at the end of a three-hour hike. We can breathe again.

Understanding: Transporting to inside others

Vacation: Escape from responsibility

Bob, from Burlingame, California, hits the road with his fifth-wheel trailer to get away from it all.

Everything is arranged. A neighbor will get the mail, a friend will water houseplants, and motel reservations are waiting. We're packed, got snacks, got gas. It's off to breakfast to start our vacation with OJ, bacon, and waffles. As we leave town, both yelling "Adios!" at the exact same time, we put in our favorite tape and take a deep breath. Good-bye, responsibilities. Hello, freedom.

Realizing a dream vacation

I'd dreamed of tropical beaches all my life and imagined how my body would feel slipping into warm, crystal blue water, where I could still see my toes. I'd seen these beaches on the cover of brochures lots of times, and a travel page out of *Sunset* magazine had been on the refrigerator for years. Whenever I was in travel agencies, booking a flight to Denver or Tulsa, I'd fantasized about all the places displayed on the wall, such as Hawaii, the Caribbean, or Tahiti. Then one day the agent told me places like that weren't just for rich people. My world changed.

Now here I am. My bank account's gone, but wow—the brochures weren't lying. Just looking at the white beach and clear water takes my breath away. Must be what heaven looks like.

Going anywhere breaks routine. Caribbean cruises drain bank accounts, but camping or just plain lounging around and gabbing all provide a free pause—the magic bullet that perks us up. European art galleries and tropical beaches are standard destinations for those of us who have saved for a "real vacation," but camping, hiking, or water skiing fits more budgets. Rich people go on safari in Africa, while just-making-it folks settle for Budget Motel overnight. Those of us in between save up for Disneyland or a few days in Mexico.

Whether vacation time means a hideaway for two in a mountain cabin or Wallyworld for six, we keep on coming back for more—even when things go wrong; who could forget sleeping on the airport floor for six hours, or when downpour finally soaked through the tent at Yellowstone. Then there's the trip when Dick drank the water when friends warned against it.

Satisfying the nomad in us can be the adventure of taking off on a road trip with no destination in mind, or a carefully choreographed tour of twenty-three states, where we know the when and where and how of every single hour. Negotiating a trip when a nomad and a homebody travel together makes for lively discussion . . . and sometimes cancellation fees on a credit card.

Having small children locks us into certain kinds of travel—usually camping or relatives or amusement parks. It's just easier. But children grow up and options multiply; attention spans lengthen, bladders get tougher, and savings accounts grow. Eventually we can graduate from camp cot to oceanfront suite in Maui. Dropping the kids off at Grandma's for a week and going back to an empty house means relaxed, uninterrupted conversations and a rare chance for romance.

Two weeks in Paris, two days at a B&B, two hours at the movies, or two minutes in meditation—it's all a vacation for your mind. It's freedom from *having* to do anything. Freedom from obligations, decisions, and worries means a break from the sameness.

On travel: Leaving here for there opens your eyes.

Consider staying close to home. Nearby areas may be worlds apart from where you live.

Walk: Free tour of nature

Kathleen, from Grants Pass, Oregon, takes a brisk four-mile walk in the rain to unwind.

Thirty extra pounds started me walking at first, but gradually I began to notice things along the way. My route is in the country, so there's a lot to see, and it constantly changes. Sometimes there's a squirrel to talk to, horses perk up their ears and nicker, and there's a look that only a cow can give. They have that stare, that dumbfounded look, when you pass. Cats stare with wary eyes, and dogs are too busy barking to make any eye contact at all.

Most days part of my walk is along a stream, which changes with the seasons. After a winter storm it's rushing and high, but it barely moves in the spring, making a gurgle that I love. One day I started a game with myself by making a little boat from a scrap of black plastic that was stuck to a rock. I nudge it along every morning to see where it ends up by the next day.

In the fall, leaves crinkle under my feet, but this breaks the silence, so I go out of my way to walk on pine needles. They're like a soft, quiet carpet, which makes me feel like an Indian tracking his dinner through the woods.

Being a surveyor for fifteen years has made me a ground watcher, so I'm always noticing the details that other people miss, such as little tree frogs or lizards trying to get out of the way.

Walking exercises brain cells along with body parts. Absorbing the passing scene silently adds to memories; taking this time to mull adds insight. Walking takes us away—from our house, our chaos, and our worries—and is so handy, so adaptable. We can take a brisk two-miler by ourselves or give our tot a treat by pushing a stroller. We can go 'round in circles at the mall or along side waves at the beach; wear holey sweats or designer outfits.

Walkers relieve the stress of both mind and body, but sometimes it just gets them to where they want to go. Parking eight blocks away from work lets us fit our exercise into a hectic schedule. It doesn't really matter where we walk, and it doesn't matter why. It only matters *that* we do.

After years of pitching weights and workouts for fitness, health journal advice finally slowed down to plain and simple walking. Simple, unless you have to walk past loose dogs defending their space. An old golf club's good for this.

Walking unique: In the snow at night

Walking increases circulation. Muscles and blood vessels in your legs act like a pump, boosting blood back up to your heart.

Watching: Just look

*Karin, from Medford, Oregon, calms her
inner being at the ocean.*

I'd spent plenty of time at the beach over the years, watching the surf pound the sand. The constant roar and rhythm of the waves hypnotized me. Watching the continual surging always calmed my mood. And when I needed an energy boost, I came during winter storms to get face to face with nature. The raging power of the ocean literally screamed in my face. Sometimes I screamed back.

Today was different. I crouched in a rock crevice and watched the ocean from a different angle. The sea was barely visible—I was tucked in a niche of granite that blocked my view—but every so often a big wave came crashing around and through this collection of eroded boulders. Even though I knew it was coming, I jumped every time. The roar, the turbulence, the wondering if I'll get drenched all added to the adventure. When an extra-powerful wave reached out for my feet, I felt like applauding its success in getting through the maze. It was as if the sea had been trying all that time to reach me. I spent most of the day just sitting and staring at that opening, waiting for another big one.

Dedicated wave watchers slip away to the beach every chance they get. The constant motion hypnotizes their senses, temporarily muting the stress of their everyday lives. But those of us with fantasy to spare look upward for our inspiration; devoted sky watchers lie on the grass to watch clouds silently morph from one species to another.

We're surrounded by eyefuls, such as art galleries, bird-baths, sunsets, soccer games, or the lush of a manicured golf course. One man's comfort, however, can be another man's nightmare, like roses in bloom. Sneezers dread those first signs of spring.

Nothing beats snuggling down by a January fire to warm icy toes, but it's the sight of dancing flames that completes our pleasure. "A sight for sore eyes" conjures up images of found puppies, toddlers, and long-lost friends. In fact, there's a lot of that at the airport. Veteran watchers amuse themselves by making up stories about why all those travelers are so happy to see each other.

Hummingbirds make everyone pause. They're so little. How on Earth do they flap so fast? And how do they aim such a long beak into the tiny hole of a feeder without bumping the side by mistake? The fluorescent pink of their throats glistens in the sunlight, and if you're sitting inside, you can watch them hover at the window, mistaking your vase of flowers for breakfast. If you sit very still outside, and wear something red, they'll hum right up to 6 inches from your face and look you in the eye.

Water: See it, hear it, drink it, play in it

Don, from Sutter Creek, California, wades in a cold stream on a hot day after he's had a drink of it.

The afternoon temperature had been frying my brain, and the weatherman had guaranteed another 100-degree day. I wasn't going to spend a third day pretending I was five and running through the sprinklers in my backyard, so by noon I was at the lake. By the time I hiked down the bank and found a flat spot for my blanket, I could almost taste the dip I was about to take. It was so hot that, with my eyes closed, I could imagine how the witch in Hansel and Gretel felt after that push.

I hurried to the edge and just kept going. That first touch didn't even alter my pace—no time to whine about that first chill. As the water level crept up to envelop all of me, my body whispered, "Ahhh."

Come summertime, when the living is hot, water calls. Some of us get crabbier and crabbier, as the hot days pass, until we get our fix. An afternoon swim or even wading in a stream satisfies for just a little while, until the heat cranks us up once again.

Water revives us, inside and out, and connects all our senses. You can sip from a mountain creek or just listen to it gurgle. You can quietly watch it bubbling over rocks, or splash the kids while you remember the water balloons and squirt gun fights when you were younger. Best of all, feel the cool against your hot skin. Water has it all.

Cities all over the world spend a fortune on elegant fountains in their public squares because they know water sounds soothe. But like a tiger, which can also gently carry her cubs by their heads, water can be fierce. Witness the Grand Canyon. Water works.

Wheelchair Accessible: Getting in—and out—of everyday places

For my cousin Doug, from Fremont, California, relief is seeing this sign.

My imagination refused to go where it has never been. The following is excerpted from my interview with Doug. To preserve his extraordinary wit, I merely massaged his account ever so slightly.

My legs stopped working eight years ago, and I started using a manual wheelchair. While I no longer stand or walk, I find that my need to use a toilet now and then continues undiminished. So it is always with great relief that I locate a handicapped accessible toilet. Last night was no exception.

After dinner, I rolled off to find the bathroom. No easy task in this restaurant. As I followed the signs down the hall I wondered if this would be my lucky night, or would I have to hold it—again—until we got home. Nope, no such luck.

Some owners, of even fancy restaurants, are under the

impression that "accessible" means a wheelchair just has to fit through the door, and then it's home free. Wrong. Fortunately, I have the upper body strength of an orangutan and can maneuver myself, using Spiderman gymnastics, from the door of the stall to the toilet seat. Now I just hoped that nobody would come in because, even though my chair is right next to the toilet, I can't close the stall door.

Next week, we'll eat at a place up the street. To restaurant owners who provide handicap accessible toilets, I am eternally grateful. To those who don't, "May your plumbing back up."

Until you actually navigate in a wheelchair yourself, how would you know? How could you possibly know what's it like? It's sort of like having children; there's no way to describe that feeling of attachment. You have to do it yourself.

Establishments comply with the law and do A, B, and C, but until the owner tests the route to the pot, *and up again*, he has to depend on his customers to speak up. By then he's done his alterations and isn't about to rip them apart. Maybe taking Wheelchair 101 for a day before calling a contractor would help. Community organizations sometimes offer this course — Handicap Awareness Day — when the walking navigate around town in a chair all day, testing wheelchair accessibility to everywhere.

The truth is most of us just haven't had much practice interacting with wheelchairs. After all, how many do we see in a day? In small towns, not even every week. Come out, come out, wherever you are. Let us know you.

Wheelchair access: Brings a new meaning to that phrase our grandmothers used—"Comfort Station."

Writing: Fingers channeling brainwaves

Stacy, from Seattle, Washington, writes poetry and then reflects on it with great satisfaction.

Every morning I let it all out by writing it down. Evidently, I have a lot to purge this morning because I was awake from 2:00 to 4:00 last night . . . thinking. I got up an hour before everyone else in the house to relieve my mind with my pen.

My favorite china coffee cup, with its lavender pansies and paper-thin lip, is in my left hand. The smoothest of smooth writing pens is in my right. My tablet is open and I'm off. This time I'm scribbling so fast I can't read my own handwriting. But I don't need to; I just need to spill my brains onto the paper. In half an hour I've filled five pages of . . . almost gibberish. Now I can start my real day.

Even when there's someone to talk to, writing it down seems different. Maybe our brain doesn't believe it until it's in black and white. True, having a person to share with decreases finger cramps and pencil dependency, but written words magically transform audio into visual.

Things seem more real once we see the words. Dedicated journalers already know this; they do it every day. Writing before sleep defuses our daily mental cache, making sure our dreams are lighter; maybe then we can fly or dance or sing. Writing before the day starts lubricates our mind and gets it rolling for the day—clears out cobwebs left over from dream frustrations and fears the night before.

Physically writing the words forces us to slow down and go over feelings again. It helps us figure them out, especially if we do it slowly enough to maintain the meticulous penmanship our grade school teachers taught us.

Of course, for those of us who love stringing words together, writing brings a special kind of satisfaction. Some words couple so nicely together—they roll right off your tongue—that we relish in their just-rightness.

A fine writing instrument—a pen with just the right feel for you—puts the pleasure in writing. Good jobs require good tools. Ask a carpenter.

X-Tra Time: Doing less to experience more

For Eric, from Dallas, Texas, free time is recess.

It's Saturday and no alarm clock. There's time to laze around in bed, dozing on and off for as long as I want. Nothing is planned for after that, so I have time to actually enjoy breakfast. Hmmm, what to do for the day. Whatever it is can be at my own pace because I've got the whole day to *not look* at the clock.

Maybe I just want to sit still and empty my mind.
Maybe I just want to sit and watch . . . flies fly.

A rare treat: not having to be anywhere at any certain time, to do what we feel like doing for as long as we want, not having to do it in any certain way. Without time limits we could linger over coffee with a friend, have breakfast at ten, or sit on the floor and play with the kids.

There's never enough time for some of us. We try cramming too much into every hour, as if our value was defined by a tally sheet of daily accomplishments. But for those of us who yearn for more calm, planning less to do every day, and giving everything we plan more time, is a great beginning.

Next time the grocery store checker apologizes for the delay say, "No problem. I'm not in a hurry." Then watch the relief on her face. You just made her day.

Happiness is never having to hurry.
Did you know that slower is better when you vacuum?
Gives it time to suck up more dirt.

Yard Work: A chance to nurture

For Carol, from Grants Pass, Oregon, time stops when she sits quietly in the corner of a well-kept garden.

My dad loved his garden and it showed. There wasn't a weed in sight as you walked along the path that wound through his flowers and trees. My sister and I carved our initials in the corner of a checkerboard patio, where each square was lovingly poured, troweled, and then sprinkled with color. I even helped smooth red into many of them myself.

I thought I knew what *orderly* meant by the time I grew up, but today I went to a Japanese garden and my definition changed.

Passing through that first archway was like stepping into another world. I never knew you could put up a doorway outside where there are no walls. Those mini-passageways always introduced another section of perfection. The surprise overhangs and buildings scattered around were stopping areas where you could pause to enjoy a new section of plants. You could always tell who the regulars were—their eyes were closed in meditation.

Even though no gardeners were in sight, my fantasy was of a hundred nimble Japanese fingers, meticulously pruning, pulling, and planting. The fact that everything was in just the "right" spot, made me speculate that weeds have learned not to bother growing here.

Besides scrumptious veggies, yard work connects us with nature, and maybe a mud pie or two. The constant change that seasons bring keeps us on our toes with the hoes. Keeping roses healthy despite the perils of prickles and pests keeps us interested. And when a prized clematis withers from mysterious forces, gardening turns into a challenge.

Vegetable gardeners in the country do a special dance with their does during the growing season. The deer, standing as still as statues, look like they're waiting in the wings for handouts . . . or maybe an open gate. Definitely a Norman Rockwell moment.

True gardeners don't care about manicures or insects. (Bumblebees are smart enough to know we're not flowers.) They notice every single weed that clutters their handiwork, and for visitors, they proudly spout off the Latin names.

Just 5 minutes of tending can ease our tension. It's the nurturing, the constant change, and the time out from the mental work of the day that brings us comfort. Bottom line is that most of us relish taking care of something; and plants don't bark or leave land mines to clean up or step into.

TLC is evident in a yard where every corner has been carefully planned.

The meticulous precision of a Japanese garden automatically brings us down and sucks us into a world of calm; a garden bursting with color lifts our spirits; and ferny, moist grottos cool our senses.

Many of us can remember that unkempt jungle of weeds up the block when we were growing up (our parents always dubbed it a rental), but the lawn surrounding the mansion on the hill seems just a little too perfect. We can almost imagine the browbeaten gardener cutting every blade with fingernail scissors, and wonder if he's getting paid enough.

Japanese garden: The opposite of chaos

A Garden Retreat

Create a space in your yard where worries aren't allowed. Start with a special entrance and personalize it by giving it a name. Devise a sitting area: add spots of color, plants that attract wildlife, and water if you can. Walking through the entrance will soon be a signal for your brain to turn off.

Young at Heart: Keeps you in the loop

For Irene, from Tacoma, Washington, feeling younger than she is keeps her involved with life.

My ninetieth birthday was today. I can't believe it. When did I get so old? My joints remind me every morning at 7:30, but my brain still says I'm sixty; I think it stopped counting the years about that time.

I had my hair done this morning because my grandchildren were coming over to take me out to dinner. My beautician started my day off by saying she always thought I was seventyish. Now I really did feel twenty years younger . . . but still planned on taking a nap.

By the time my grandchildren came, I was raring to go. It was wonderful to watch them chatter. My granddaughter has a new pet—a rabbit she rescued in a parking lot. My grandson just bought a motorcycle. And he brought an extra helmet. I could tell that even though he brought the helmet he didn't really think I'd do it and was surprised when I answered yes. I surprised myself.

They both smiled as I carefully lifted the helmet over my head (I just had my hair done). It was much lighter than it looked. No one had a camera, thank goodness, as I lifted my leg higher than I had in years to swing it over the back. I held on tight to my grandson as we rode around the block and up the street and back. I felt so alive! Of course, getting off was another story.

Those five minutes shaved another ten years from my age. I could tell by their laughter that they were actually having a good time with their old grandma. I'm so grateful that they want to share their lives with me.

As I get in bed tonight, I feel like fifty. OK . . . maybe sixty.

Feeling younger than the years we've accumulated keeps us included . . . in our children's and grandchildren's lives and in the world around us. Figuring out what comes first is the tough part, because the young-at-heart circle feeds on itself. Curiosity drives us to keep informed; being informed stimulates our interest; having more interests makes us more interesting, and so on.

The fact that our culture worships youth feeds our egos when we're mistaken for younger than we are. Revlon, plastic surgeons, and health clubs make sure we all want to go backward after our eyes and breasts hit forty years. But it's a positive attitude, not tighter skin and flatter bellies, that keeps us current on the latest fads and lingoes.

Keeping both our minds *and* our bodies fit brings us better health, and better health motivates us to stay there. The circle grows into itself, so anywhere we can jump on draws us into the loop. And the momentum carries us along, past eighty, past ninety.

Sometime after thirty, some of us just stop aging and continually slip back to twenty-five in our minds. Oh, we know the truth by Friday at 6:00 P.M. or when we get out of bed at 7:00 A.M., but our twenty-five-year-old exuberance keeps our hearts young.

A continuum: Positive attitude > more interests > clearer mental activity > greater physical action > better health > fewer wrinkles > positive attitude > more interests > and so on

ZZZs: Renew and reactivate

Caroline, from Medford, Oregon, replenishes her energy overnight.

My bed has been calling me all day. It's been calling this sleep-deprived body to lie down and catch up. I didn't realize how tired I was until I looked at myself in the mirror. Bag city. Then I looked back on the weekend; I was too busy having fun on Saturday night to ever look at the clock, and it was midnight before I noticed how late it was. Then on Sunday night I got hooked on a long TV movie and was too keyed up to fall asleep for hours.

So, now it's Monday, and by three o'clock I turned into one of those clock-watching employees. By the time I was in the car heading home, all I could think about was my bed. This body yearned to lie down, to collapse and close burning eyes. By the time dinner was over, my bed was screaming at me. I called back, "Coming, bed."

The end of the day is when we get to replace binding daytime clothes with nothing . . . or almost. Aaaah, to get prone, take a deep breath, and finally close our eyes for the day is heavenly. Every muscle moans, "Thanks." The pause that refreshes is sleep. Even a 10-minute rest relieves scratchy eyes and a sagging spirit.

Sleep refreshes mind and body and invites lavish and outlandish dreams. Sharing nighttime entertainment with a partner starts the day off with a good laugh, although capturing them is tricky; it's important to start talking as soon as our eyes open.

Some of us wear earplugs every night so we can stay next to a snoring partner; we're taught that it's the proper place to be if we're really happy with each other. Frankly, that time is too valuable to put up with a noisy partner, so moving to another room can keep us sane. Besides, playing musical beds adds extra interest to relationships.

Researchers say that most of us these days go through life sleep deprived. Makes you wonder how different things would be if everyone slept more: fewer car crashes, more smiles, longer tempers, and lots of disappointed therapists.

Sleep: Hitting the snooze button at 6:00 A.M. allows for one more 7-minute dream.

Appendix

On Stress

I'm often surprised by my own fears. I realize, during moments of reflection, that these are what keep me from living my life to the fullest. If I take the time to examine each one, almost all of them are irrational, irrelevant, and debilitating. All my life I've worried about everything, and in the end, most of it never really mattered.

To get an idea of why we need to be comforted, everyone in the survey was asked about the personal stresses in their own life. The following verbatim list of what they revealed to me confirms that none of us is alone.

Coping: # 1 Stress
- Adapting to life as a widow
- Strained relationship with spouse due to remodeling
- Life
- Marital difficulties
- Depression
- Not having friends and family around day to day
- Isolation
- Lack of intimacy
- Daily survival
- Not being "first" on anyone's list

- Caring for three grandchildren
- Living next door to mother-in-law
- Still having to work—I'm tired
- Getting through the days and nights—boring
- Learning to cope with being at home with no kids
- A husband who works all the time
- Talk of retirement—I don't want change
- Dealing with effects of husband's stroke—more changes than I thought
- Impatience of growing old and the slowdown that comes with it
- School—grades
- Not being with my mom—I miss her
- Reflecting to see what I need to do to improve myself
- Being on my own for the first time
- Finding the right woman
- Getting behind in work—trying to get caught up
- The holidays
- Gaining weight
- The thought of moving to another house
- Death of a loved one
- Major changes at work
- Not being in control
- Making mistakes at my job
- Slow pace at work

- Losing my best friend and partner after forty years of marriage
- Not doing the work I love to do—not feeling fulfilled
- Remodeling—cooking and eating in a dinky motor home for months
- Phone calls at dinnertime asking for money
- What to make for dinner that's healthy and that my kids will eat
- No good shopping in this town
- Constant laundry
- Not being able to help someone who won't help themselves
- Preparing the house for out-of-town visitors
- Trying to downsize and simplify our lives
- Wishing my wife would stop smoking
- Finding that final place to live that will make my wife happy
- Building a new house
- The unfairness of life to children and the elderly

Health

- Worrying about my mom's health
- Granddaughter's surgery
- Bad health
- Deteriorating health of friends and people my age

- Being sick with flu
- TMJ and arthritis in my jaw
- Concern over husband's health
- Bum foot that limits walking
- Aching hips
- Healing from recent surgery
- Keeping fit as I age
- The health of our nation
- Dealing with health care system, insurance, doctors, hospitals, and prescription prices
- My father's health
- Ongoing disability
- Work, school, DMV

General

- Evil people
- People who argue, especially about politics
- Clients who don't show up on time
- Stupid people
- Complainy people
- Poor international relations and risk of world wars

Money

- Starting my own business—not having a weekly paycheck
- Possibility of losing my job
- Figuring out how to invest for retirement security

- Difficulty in growing my own business
- Money—not enough of it
- Paying for all the hats that I love
- Refinancing our house
- Holiday money—lack
- The economy/world stability
- Having a stack of unpaid bills and only $5 in the bank
- Stretching that paycheck to cover all my bills and be able to eat
- Retirement money
- Tight finances

Children

- Grown son returning to live at home
- Worry about my grown children
- Child abuse
- Kids!!! (a two-year-old screamer and a teenager)
- Learning to let go of adult children
- My children growing up on me

Time

- Not enough time for comforts
- Piles of student papers to read and grade
- Thinking that I need to get things done that are not really important
- Too little time to do what I enjoy

- Too much to do at work and home
- Too many things that need to get done, not enough time

No Stress

- "No stress, just chaos."
- "And this too shall pass away. . . ."

Acknowledgment and Thanks

A heartfelt thanks to all the faithful respondents to my survey. This project would not exist without them!

Byron & Margie Baxley
Diana Bergen
Rebecka Binning
Don Bishop
Dan & Yvonne Bower
Bob & Sue Cossins
Linda Doig
Joe Dunbar
Doug & Paula Eads
Jan Fahr
Suzi Francis
Debra Gebhard
Betty & Phillip Gooch
Linda Gorham
Dorothy Hansen
Roland Hassel
Robyn Hawk
Kathy & Roy Headley
Josh Headley
Matt Headley

Cynthia Hewitt
Dylan Hewitt
Isobel Holt
Gloria Irwin
Pam Kelly
Eletheah Kesarah
Chris Kiltz
Dena Knight
Kathy Krauss
Donna Lakin
Anne & Hank
    Leenknecht
Craig Lighty
Carol Lippert
Judy & Don Liston
Adrienne & Tom
    Logsdon
Bill & Karen Long
Irene & Jim Lowman
Peggy Malone

Susan McKenzie

Elizabeth O'Bryan

Sue Orris

Karin Penn

Shauna Richardson

Jerry & Joanne
    Robertson

Judy Rodriguez

Kathy Roesner

Diane Rogers

Linda Rudisill

Chris Ruppel

Seattle Goth
    Community

Nancy & Tim Schmidt

Kelly Schmidt

Eric Schmidt

Kimberly Sellers

Lorol Simmons

Gail Smith

Christina Spencer

Kellie Stone

Serena Ota St. Clair

Pan Tangible

Donna Vocke

Joey Ward

Stu Watson

Kathy & Joe Weaver

Pat Webb

Bill Wiseman

Christy Wiseman

Jean Wiseman

Jesse Wiseman

And those who preferred to remain anonymous:

Abigail	Jennie
Alice	Jerri
Alison	Joan
Anita	John
Bethany	Linda
Blake	Lyndsey
Bobby	Mark
Buck	Mary Anne
Carmen	Maryann
Carrie	MaryLou
Carrie	Melanie
Charles	Pauline
Charlotte	Rich
Cleo	Sally
Connie	Stacy
Cynthia	Susie
Dennis	Teresa
Diane	Walter
Jeff	Willie

To Our Readers

Conari Press, an imprint of Red Wheel/Weiser, publishes books on topics ranging from spirituality, personal growth, and relationships to women's issues, parenting, and social issues. Our mission is to publish quality books that will make a difference in people's lives—how we feel about ourselves and how we relate to one another. We value integrity, compassion, and receptivity, both in the books we publish and in the way we do business.

Our readers are our most important resource, and we value your input, suggestions, and ideas about what you would like to see published. Please feel free to contact us, to request our latest book catalog, or to be added to our mailing list.

Conari Press
An imprint of Red Wheel/Weiser, LLC
P.O. Box 612
York Beach, ME 03910-0612
www.conari.com